Asha Miró

The Other Face of the Moon

Finding my Indian Family

institut
ramon llull

summersdale

THE OTHER FACE OF THE MOON

First published in two volumes as *La Filla del Ganges* and *Les Dues Cares de la Lluna* in the Catalan language by Edicions La Magrana S.A. in 2003 and 2004.

This edition published in 2006 by Summersdale Publishers Ltd.

English Translation by Jamal Mahjoub, © Summersdale Publishers Ltd and Simon & Schuster, Inc. The translation of this book was supported by the Institut Roman Llull.

LLLL institut
ramon llull

Summersdale Publishers Ltd
46 West Street
Chichester
West Sussex
PO19 1RP
UK

www.summersdale.com

Printed and bound in Great Britain.

ISBN 1 84024 495 X

The
Other Face
of the Moon

Contents

Part 1. Daughter of the Ganges

1. My First Trip Back to India 8

2. Bombay 21

3. Nine Instead of Five 28

4. The Bread of Necessity 33

5. The Spiral Staircase 43

6. Something to Offer 64

7. Mary 70

8. The Rear Entrance 77

9. An Object of Attention 87

10. Films and Injections 94

11. Nasik 103

12. Back From India 119

Part 2. The Other Face Of The Moon

1. Returning to my Origins.................................128

2. Everything in its Proper Place.............................133

3. Seeing Mumbai with New Eyes 145

4. Usha and the Sacred City................................154

5. Daughters of the Godavari 168

6. Sitabai and Sakabai...................................196

7. My Sister Asha's Story.....................................212

8. Leaving the Land Behind 230

Notes...236

Glossary of Indian Words 237

Acknowledgements 241

Part One:

Daughter

of the Ganges

1

My First Trip Back to India

Six thirty in the morning and I can't have slept for more than two hours. I leap out of bed, switch off the alarm and jump straight into the shower. I gaze at the swirling water as it washes away, looking for any trace of the images in my dreams, the nervous build-up to the journey, and the worries I have about how it might affect the life I have become accustomed to, a way of life that continues out of simple habit. Hot water and soap are not going to be enough to make a clean start. The time has come for me to turn back, to relive my early childhood years, to go forward by breaking with my life as it is now. It is time to go back to India.

I am returning to India because that is where I was born, on the 7th of November, 1967. I lived there until the age of six, when I was adopted by the two people whom I know today as my parents. I know that I came into this world at a place called Nasik, in the west of the country. I know too that I spent my early years in an orphanage in Bombay. Apart from that I know little for certain. That is the reason for this journey, to try to address a long series of questions.

The days prior to my departure have been an endless succession of goodbyes. More than one person has brought up the million dollar question: Are you sure you are ready for this, Asha? Each time, I nodded my head silently with the same instinctive gesture, so as not to give any sign of the doubts which have been nagging at me. The two people I could never fool – I wouldn't even try – are my parents.

In my room, I brush out my long black hair in front of the mirror. I put a touch of mascara above my black eyes, just as I do every morning. It is going to be a long journey and I want to be sure I'll be comfortable. I pick out a long skirt with blue and white flowers, a white teeshirt and my old sandals. Actually, it's the best skirt I have; I want to make an impression when I arrive back in my country. While I am dressing I run a mental check over everything that I have packed in my rucksack: a pair of loose, lightweight trousers, and a pile of teeshirts and underwear so as not to give away how inept I am when it comes to laundry. I also have another pair of sandals with thick soles for walking, and a collection of recommended pharmaceuticals, tablets with impossible names that I have to take to avoid malaria and other illnesses. I also have mosquito repellent. In another, smaller rucksack, I have my camera, a notebook, pens, paints, sketchbook, passport, vaccination certificate and dollars. The notebook I shall use as a diary. I have never kept one before, but I want to be sure to write down everything that happens to me, all my impressions. I don't want anything to be left out.

I say farewell to my flat, the balcony full of geraniums, and the spires of the Sagrada Familia sticking up between the opposite buildings. Fatima is going to take care of the geraniums for the month that I am away. Fatima is my sister. She too was born in India, though at the other end of the country. She arrived in Barcelona a few months ahead of me, at the age of only a year and a half. We are truly sisters, united not by the bond of sharing the same biological parents, but by something that is equally or more indestructible: the affection of parents who brought us together and raised us as they would have done their own daughters. Our parents converged our separate paths into one, allowing us to share the adventure of belonging to the same family.

Four weeks from now those spires will not have moved. One or two geraniums might have withered and other new flowers will have sprung up in their place. I, on the other hand, will no longer be the same. I have a feeling that something inside me will change forever.

⋇⋇

Twenty years after that first journey – which brought me from Bombay to Barcelona – I am aboard a plane that will take me to where I hope to find the answers to a huge number of questions, to shed a little light on the uncertainty, to fill in the missing pieces of my reality.

Destination: Bombay.

The engines are warming up and the aircraft starts to roll forward as we pick up speed for take-off. A prayer rises from deep inside me as we climb up into the sky, so close to heaven, touching the one who has singled me out and guided me to precisely this point. I ask for the strength to see me through this task and for the courage to go on, to stay the course, to follow it through to the end and not fail; to find the inner peace that I want so much and finally to set aside the doubts that have been bothering me.

Beneath us everything grows smaller and smaller until it resembles one of those pointillist paintings that I love so much. I can still make out the pinnacles of the church spires. Seen from the air, my beloved Barcelona looks even more beautiful. The distinctive lines of the Eixample are perfectly defined. The leaves of the trees which follow the Rambla lose themselves in the waves, the blues and greens flowing together into a single tone in the pale sun, dissolving the distinct outline of the contours into a gentle silhouette.

Sitting in the turquoise blue seat of the Air India plane, I am a bundle of nerves as I try to recall what that little girl of six (almost seven) might have been thinking, sitting in a turquoise seat just like this one, as she made that journey in reverse; the journey that dropped her into the arms of a family which, up until then, had only been a sense of longing to her, in the shape of a black and white photograph. I feel sure I must have passed the long hours scribbling in a drawing book with the crayons given to me by a hostess – as elegant in her sari as the one who now comes to serve me lunch.

❃

At home, we have always talked of India, my country, the place where I was born. Whenever there was a programme on television about it we would all get together on the sofa – Dad, Mum, Fatima, and me – and sit there glued to it. A documentary that gave some insight into a stunning landscape and the people who lived there, the poverty they were fated to live in, would often lead us to talk about our childhood and how my sister and I had arrived in Barcelona from the same country but at different times; what it had been like for my parents to adopt two children; how they had managed to get through all the paperwork, all of which had to be written in Spanish and then translated into English, a language neither of them spoke; and of the anxiety and emotion they felt throughout all the preparations. Looking back, I know that it was very brave of them. They adopted us in the early 1970s, when it wasn't a common choice to make. They must have felt very much alone, unable to share their worries with anyone. This is another reason why I shall always admire them. Those evenings spent on the sofa gave us an ideal opportunity to talk about the adoption. It was done in such a simple way that it became another facet of our life together. Those talks always arrived at the same conclusion: since we could not remember much about the country we came from, we always agreed that one day we would all go back there together. For us girls it would be a return to our country, while for them it would be a chance to get to know the country that had given them two daughters.

The years went by but the right moment never seemed to present itself; if it wasn't one thing it was another. Finally, I reached the point where I felt that I was ready, that I wanted to go back to my country. However, for me, the return itself was as important as the way in which I made the journey. I couldn't just fly out there like an ordinary tourist. I couldn't quite see myself walking into a travel agency to flick through the holiday brochures and pick out the nicest hotels and choose a promising itinerary. No, that wasn't the idea at all. Knowing the reality of India, I wasn't going to settle for just passing through the country, passively taking in the view. I wasn't going to India to visit majestic palaces and temples, to cross valleys and mountains, or to try my hand at bargaining while shopping for souvenirs. In Barcelona, in my second life, I had been given everything: a family, friends, an education – all in all, a life of complete freedom. I couldn't go back with my hands empty. Inside I was torn between my feelings of belonging to India and the equally intense feeling of alienation. I was expecting to arrive in a country that would reflect my character, yet a place where destiny had decided I was not to grow up, because I had been chosen out of millions of other children. I have always been aware that I was privileged to be singled out. This thought is constantly present and often has me asking: why me? The answer has always been an overwhelming silence. Fate took a hand in the game and I feel like a tiny piece on the board marked for preferential treatment. Unless you decide to ignore the world around you, this is not an easy label to bear. I have always avoided the gaze of those Indians you meet on the street or in restaurants, trying to sell you a rose. In all these years, whenever I come face to face with that familiar dark, penetrating gaze, I never know where to look. I am never able to look them squarely in the eye. It is especially at these times that the question of why I was chosen comes back to me, and the feelings of disquiet make their presence felt even more powerfully.

Fate was to play its part again when I came across the information folder of an NGO called Setem that described a volunteer work camp in India. The same hand of fate ensured that, in the vast country of India, this project happened to be located in Bombay, the city where I lived in an orphanage from the age of three until I was six. To make it even more perfect, I discovered that there was a Setem work camp in Nasik, the city washed by the sacred waters of the Godavari, where I had first opened my eyes. It was my dream, presented on a silver platter. But since I have never had much luck winning anything, I filled in the form without getting my hopes up too high. A couple of months later I received a letter telling me that I had made it through the first round and would be required to attend an interview. It was all beginning to come together. Up until that point I had kept it all secret, dealing with my anxiety alone, convinced that nothing would come of it. I didn't want to worry my parents unnecessarily. All I had was the complicity of my boyfriend, who supported me with whatever I did. Once I had completed the interview and it was confirmed that I could join the work camp, I realised it was time to tell everyone at home.

My parents sat on the sofa and I on the small wooden stool. It was always the same when we had to discuss something really important. I came out with it all at once, anxious but excited, attentive to every gesture, to each reaction. I needed those eyes, fixed on me with concern, to give me their blessing, to assure me that they would be with me no matter how far away I was. Their little girl was going to India, all on her own! My parents had always assumed that this would be a family project, involving all of us; they didn't think that it might awaken something in me, that I might take the initiative without them. In fact, however, my decision did not take them completely by surprise. Deep in their hearts they were sure I would follow my own path and knew I would have to learn about the place that had given me this brown skin. But their concern never led them to express their feelings aloud, for fear that this might make it come true. Despite their worries, I was very much aware of the adventure I had embarked upon. I would need to be determined if I wanted to fill the gap of those first seven years, which I had left so far behind me.

Questions and more questions, fired off with such speed that I didn't even have time to answer. All at once I flung myself between them and they both put their arms around me. I felt safe there between the strength of my father's arms and the calm of my mother's, just as I had so many times before over the years. Wrapped in my father's arms I would play that game all children love: to reach up and touch an infinite imaginary heaven, even if only with the tips of my fingers. He doesn't know this, but even today, when no one is watching, I stand on my balcony and raise my hands towards the sky, up towards the seagulls flying over my beloved Barcelona. I ask them to lift me up for an instant so I can touch heaven.

My mother's arms taught me the laws that rule the heart and the spirit. To love, to offer consolation, to cry for your own pain or that of others. To soothe hatred, while allowing the best of oneself to flow. Neither of them spared an ounce of effort in trying to give us, my sister as much as myself, everything we needed and more. They may not have given us the breath of life, but they had given us the essentials, and with the same care as a potter molds his clay, they had formed us into people.

I am often shaken by the excessive importance many people place on being related by blood. Obviously, it has a certain importance. But so does everything that comes afterwards, all that my parents have given me, a legacy which goes beyond blood.

My parents were worried about me; they didn't like to think that they would not be there during my journey to lend a hand, to soothe me when I was overcome by sadness, to help me understand everything I was going to encounter. At the same time they realised that the process of bringing me up had been completed, that everything they had given me had formed me as a person and that, consequently, I would be prepared to deal with anything. To them, I would always be their little girl, but now they could see that I had grown up.

That embrace was their blessing, to go ahead and make my journey of discovery. They gave me the energy, the strength, the drive and the courage to stay the course. I was confident that, whatever happened, they would be there for me no matter what, in the same way they had been there all those years ago, on the 27th October, at Barcelona airport, waiting on the runway, full of uncertainties. Then too, with an emotional embrace we sealed the love which has sustained us until today.

There are hours to go until we touch down in Bombay, but I have Mum's diary to keep me company. She began writing it just before I arrived in Barcelona to be her daughter. On the day I told them I was going back to India, Mum went to her room and took the notebook out of her chest of drawers, and revealed that she began to keep the diary when I came into her life. There was one for me and one for my sister, Fatima. Over all these years she had been writing to ensure that there would be a record of how things had been. She was afraid that if her memory failed she would be unable to explain these things in detail.

In giving me the diary, Mum had provided me with the tools to deal with the pain that might be waiting for me. This was my story. It wasn't a tale full of terrible secrets, because we never had any secrets at home, but there were accounts of some quite intimate episodes. During the early days, months, even years, Mum wrote every day, even if it was only a few lines. She gathered up all the daily anecdotes, the day to day of our existence, how we adapted to the new house, new family, language, food and customs.

Going through the journal for the first time, I am struck by the love my parents felt for me before we ever met. All they knew of me was what Mother Adelina had written to them from the orphanage in Bombay, and the photograph which was on their sideboard for days and days. I am very moved to realise just how much they wanted me and how much energy they put into getting me to their home. I realise that my story has a logic to it. As always, however, just as in the country I came from, it all seems contradictory. On the one hand, there are the parents who overlooked the blood ties and who wished only to make me happy from the very first instant they spoke my name. On the other hand, there is the sadness I feel thinking of those parents who didn't want me, for whom I was just a burden. And while it is also true that I tried to avoid feelings of dejection at the fact of having been rejected, I coped by thinking that there must have been a reason, some adverse circumstances that I knew nothing about. I don't really believe that they didn't want me, only that it was not in their power to take care of me. It had to be something like that.

Monday, 21ˢᵗ October, 1974

Today I went to buy this notebook with red covers in which I am going to write down each and every detail of this story of affection which is about to begin with you, our daughter Asha. I have also bought another one for Fatima, our youngest daughter, who has already been living with us for almost three months and has made our lives complete. I shall note down the little details of day to day events in each of them. In this way, when you are both grown up and my memory fails me, you will be able to know how it was for us, for your father as much as for me, when you arrived in our home.

I will be waiting for you, my dearest daughter Asha, with unbounded hopes. They have told us that you will be arriving next Sunday, the 27th October 1974, at eleven in the morning.

I could have started this diary by telling you about the months we have spent being driven mad by all the paperwork, procedures, requirements, translations... It would take ages to tell you all of that. For this reason, your father and I have decided to carefully store all the papers relating to your adoption. We went through so many unbelievable setbacks, though now all of that seems a long time ago. During the last few months we must have asked ourselves thousands of times why we chose to look in a place so far away... and it makes me laugh because there are things that you can't really explain in so many words.

We were always convinced, and as time goes by it seems even more clear, that at a certain point in our lives, four spirits coming from such distant places would grow together once and forever more.

I know that this is one of those stories I shall have to repeat to you countless times, because very soon you will become a part of it. Your father and I wanted to have the children which nature could not give us, and the two of you were clamouring for the parents you were denied by your own respective histories. Now we have come to the end of that page. It is time to turn over and start a new one, as much for you as for us.

2

Bombay

After travelling half way around the world in a matter of hours, I landed in Bombay – Mumbai, as it is now known – the Gateway of India, the city where I spent the first years of my childhood. Despite the anxiety I felt about my personal journey, I was comforted by the fact that my work camp companions shared the same hopes and aims as mine. Above all, we wanted to do something useful, to leave behind the ballast of our daily lives, lives that often seemed superficial, to feel ourselves reborn as new beings, each with all five senses keen to receive and to give.

The airport is an immense space, uninviting. The pale fluorescent lighting provides little illumination. As I walk through I try to take myself back twenty years, but the only thing I manage to remember is the glass door. It is shown in a photograph, half-blurred, which I have kept in a pocket for all these years. In it I am a tiny six year old, all dressed up, clutching the hand of the air hostess responsible for leading me towards another life. Mother Adelina is in the picture, waving goodbye, but I don't see her because I am only looking ahead. I have eyes only for my path to Barcelona. I never thought of turning to say a last farewell. It was in the moment of crossing the threshold of that glass door that I began to feel certain that I was beginning a new life. I remember feeling a strange tingling inside, a powerful mixture of happiness and regret. I must have been granted the gift of living more than one life: a reincarnation, without the physical transformation.

Tuesday, 22nd October, 1974
In these last remaining days we are desperately trying to find a school for you, so that when you arrive you can start getting used to normal daily life. Your father, as you will soon be able to see for yourself, is good with his hands and quite particular about the details. He has made some colourful cards to send to all of our friends and parents to invite them here for your arrival and 'birth' into our family. We can't keep so much joy to ourselves!

We emerge from the airport terminal. The sky is leaden and hangs heavily over us. The heat leaves us dazed and we accept as best we can the marvellous reception laid on by the people from the NGO. They hold up a welcome sign and present us with garlands of flowers. We manage to fit ourselves, along with all the rucksacks and bundles of equipment, into a minibus that will take us to the house where we will spend a couple of days until we are divided into groups and sent to stay with our respective local families. We make the journey in silence. The greyness, the stifling heat, hits us deep down, and we ask ourselves what we are doing here. I know that I can't back down. I have a challenge to meet. When I see the menacing sight of a raven brushing against the vehicle, the only thing I feel like doing is turning around and going back.

We cross the city and are struck by the poverty, the rats running along the street... The impact of our first impressions is so powerful that we are unable to really make sense of what we are seeing. Everything seems to be infused with a belief in the continuous succession of life and death, in a cycle. Here, nothing carries the same kind of importance as we give it.

According to this belief, life is simply one more step in the cycle. It will be followed by another and yet another, as long as you follow the correct path with respect to yourself and others, and do not expect any material reward for your actions. Seeing how people manage to get on with their lives under difficult conditions, without breaking down along the way, helps me put a lot of things in perspective. Of course, it would not be easy to change my way of thinking. Ideas are one thing, putting them into practice is quite another.

All of us feel a little perplexed. My companions keep an eye on me, and I feel their protective anxiety. They ask if I am all right and I reply yes, yes, of course. I don't manage to convince all of them, but I don't want them to worry. I watch the people in the streets, and it's strange to think that I was born here. I don't understand how I could have spent almost seven years of my life here. My thoughts whirl between past, present and future, and I find it hard to admit that – in some way – I am a part of these people. Evoking the past makes me wonder what my future would have been like had my life carried on as it started here. My present life, and the fact I don't know how to deal with everything around me right now, reaffirms the feeling that I was lucky to have been chosen. The smells are so overwhelming... From time to time a garden releases a delicious gust of air, but the next moment I am hit by an unexpected stench. I have my heart in my mouth.

Tuesday, 23rd October, 1974
Today's great joy has been that, thanks to a friend who works in the airport, I have managed to get a pass that will allow us to go all the way into the landing area. This way we can be waiting at the door of the plane to embrace you, receive you into our/your new family. And then all

the months of waiting will be over, the worry we have felt at not hearing any news except by letter, or brief phonecalls to the nuns. At last we will have our Asha home. I give thanks because little by little things are falling into place and everything that seemed so impossible is becoming real.

It is a couple of days since I arrived and I am finding it difficult to adapt. At times I can't avoid sinking low and thinking that I really don't know if I am going to make it. Mealtimes are some of the worst moments. I've always been a fussy eater, but since arriving here I can't manage to keep anything down, it all makes me sick. I find the food they give us too spicy and I am scared I might get ill. I feel no motivation and, since I am not eating, I can't manage to get my strength up. After supper we go up to the terrace for a while.

The stifling heat persists and the view from up there is not exactly the stuff of picture postcards: the grey sky, the sea in the background an even denser grey, the semi-derelict state of the surrounding houses, the mud, the pools of water left by the last downpour.

Despite the support of my companions who know about my fears, the process of adapting is proving to be a very steep climb. But I am not here to look at India from the rooftop of this fortress. So I gather my forces together and go to the room where Father Jordi Ribas is going to have a chat with us. I am keen to get to know him in person after all that I have heard about him. He is very charismatic and at the same time exudes a deep humility.

In even tones, and speaking from his experience, Father Jordi talks to us about an India which I have been unable to see yet, of a people driven in pursuit of their desires, who are trying to find their way, of a people full of life. He gives us a sense of what really matters in all that we see around us. How, despite the poverty, we can really get something out of this journey if we allow ourselves to be immersed in the essence of the people. In getting to know them we will learn to value the pieces that make up their lives. He underlines the importance of looking to see things in their fullness, rather than to judge. You should never judge any man until you have walked two moons in his moccasins*. The key point he makes is that we must keep our eyes wide open to grasp the exterior and arrive at the interior. There is pain, but no bitterness.

His words open a window through which we are able to see our surroundings with new eyes. He has turned us upside down and shaken out the baggage we were carrying that prevented us from recognising the harmony that exists in all things, in each person, in each gesture. First of all, no more wristwatches. We must change our way of thinking.

For me, it is the start of a new challenge: to see India the way it is, leaving aside absurd prejudices and not looking to find fault in the most obvious things – the smells, the heat, the food... I feel ready to try to understand this other India, behind which there is a whole philosophy, another reality. I needed a bit of a shove like this and it has arrived

*Old Native American saying

at the right moment, because it is now that the real journey of learning is to begin.

Thursday, 24th October, 1974

Asha, our daughter, what a happy day. Thanks to a dear friend, Pau, I have managed to get you a place in a wonderful school. For days your father and I have been round Barcelona from school to school. We were getting a little desperate because they were all giving us a hard time.

Like all parents, what we want is for you to be able to fit in, the sooner the better, and to be able to have the same kind of life as all the other boys and girls your age. We have no idea how you will take all of this. It will be difficult, as much for you as for us, but we feel confident that there will also be a good side to it all. We will learn as we go along, together.

3

Nine Instead of Five

Maria, who is the coordinator of the work camp, Núria, Gabriela and myself have been assigned to the neighbourhood of Shere Punjab. The Patil family, with whom we are lodging, receives us with open arms. I don't know who is more curious, us or them. Nadina comes out to bid us welcome. She is twelve years old and, because she speaks English very well, she is responsible for the introductions. Her father, Naresh, drives a taxi. He is a calm man of few words and exudes a great serenity. Later on, the elder daughter, Nanda, who is eighteen, arrives, and little Ibuthi, who is five, is so excited by our arrival that she runs in circles around her mother, Kamal. They all speak English, so at least there will be no problem with verbal communication. But they cannot hide their surprise at seeing me. Maria briefly tells them my story and they look at me with an affectionate smile of complicity which makes me feel very good inside.

The house is really tiny. The dining room is dominated by the television which is always on. There are decorative elements of every imaginable kind on the walls. Calendars with thick pages and striking, colourful drawings with typical Indian patterns sit in fraternal co-existence with prints of the Virgin Mary. This is where the parents and the little one sleep. Life centres around the little kitchen. On the floor there is a stone on which the mother kneads the chapatis, and in one corner an altar dedicated to Ganesh, for whom incense is burned.

Ganesh is the Hindu elephant god. He is represented as a man with a big belly and the head of an elephant. Ganesh is called upon to resolve problems and remove obstacles that come along in daily life. He is also considered a messenger between men and the gods. According to myth, Ganesh was the son of Shiva and Parvati. Shiva had to leave home when Ganesh was born and he returned years later to find a stranger barring the way into his own home. Shiva, impatient to be reunited with his wife and son, cut off the head of the guard. Parvati began to weep at this tragedy, because the guard was none other than Ganesh, who had grown up. Shiva hastily tried to make amends by cutting off the head of an elephant and placing it on the body of his son. He promised his wife that Ganesh would be a great god and men would invoke his name first when seeking to be heard by the other gods. The family that took us in calls on Ganesh with serene conviction.

We unpack our things in the room where the four of us are to sleep, with Nadina and Nanda. The room is tiny. A heap of mattresses comes out from underneath the big bed and when everything has been arranged for us to sleep, Nanda shows us around the neighbourhood.

Shere Punjab is a humble quarter of huge contrasts. To Western eyes it seems a little chaotic, but now that I am ready to start seeing from scratch, having decided to free myself of the rigid aesthetic rules I came with, I am touched by a sense of beauty that is complete in itself. In late afternoon the streets are full of life, the cheerful stalls selling fruit and spices, the smell of incense, the clothes dyed in an infinity of colours, the men smoking their bidis in the square. Time passes with no rush.

Mahakali is the name of the main street, which serves as a reference point, and Nanda shows us the route to the bus that will take us to the work camp, a school in Andheri.

Back at the house, the family presents us with what will be our very first authentic Indian supper, served with all the accompanying ritual. On the floor, on top of a mosaic of carpets and cushions, there are chapatis, rice and lentils.

It is all very spicy, but for the first time since being here I find it delicious. For the first time I manage to eat it all up without qualms; the same with having to eat using just my right hand, it's all a matter of balance, but I manage pretty well, much better than my companions. When I first arrived in Barcelona my mother found my habit of eating with my hands very amusing. Perhaps the skill has been tucked away in some corner inside me and is now resurfacing. After supper we help the children do their homework against the background of an Indian film on television, a tearful drama of the kind that lasts more than three hours, complete with obligatory old-fashioned romanticism, strident music and violence.

As we are about to go to sleep, all six of us spread out on the bed and the mattresses on the floor, I sing a lullaby for them. It is a magical moment, like a prayer. I have always adored music, ever since I was a child; I can't resist it. Then, in silence, my mind starts to go back over the day, thinking about all that has happened to me. I always do this, every night, but this time there are too many emotions, and I am just too tired to think. My eyes close involuntarily. I can think tomorrow.

Saturday, 26th October, 1974
One day before your arrival, and both your father and I are very anxious. I am writing this to you after midnight. I finally got up because I couldn't stop tossing and turning

in bed, unable to close my eyes. My thoughts are only of you, and a heap of questions are running around in my head. I know that at this precise moment you should be aboard the airplane. I worry because I can't be there with you if you feel sick or start to feel bad. It's the first time you have travelled and you are not used to the altitude. I ask myself how you must be feeling; perhaps you feel alone, but don't worry because it will be the last time, from now on you will have us and your sister, Fatima.

4

The Bread of
Necessity

Early the next morning we are awoken by the sound of the father's little bells. Naresh does his prayers, lights a stick of incense and on the doorframe he draws some flowers, different ones each day, using a whitish pigment.

Naresh is rather timid and doesn't speak a lot; the mother is more chatty and now treats me like another of her girls. She shows me how to knead the chapatis, but I am not very good with my hands. In Barcelona I was barely capable of frying an egg. With so many women gathered together in such a cramped space, everything is happiness and smiles. For breakfast we eat chapatis with jam and a mixture of tea with milk and sugar, lots of sugar. The girls are dressed in their English school uniform and look like elegant young ladies, with their hair neatly combed and their dresses carefully pressed; what is most surprising is that they appear so changed and yet are still barefoot. We get ourselves ready for what is to be our first day of work. Kamal has made lunch for us and Gabriela hands out the little packets. We are ready to go to the work camp, the Jeevan Nirwaha Niketan school (JNN).

To avoid getting lost we follow the directions that Nanda gave us yesterday and find the bus stop. We get on a bus full of schoolchildren that will take us to the JNN, in the neighbourhood of Andheri. It is an informal school and does not follow the state programme. The boys and girls who attend spend half of their day working and then spend a few hours in school. These children are often the only means of support for a family burdened with serious economic problems, not uncommonly suffering the havoc wrought by an alcoholic father. The mothers have enough work bringing up so many of children, while the children must bring in the money. They clean shoes, deliver parcels, wash cars, any job that will allow them to survive. The object of these centres is to teach basic skills in the hope that the children will be able to break out of this cycle: they learn to count so that they don't get cheated, acquire a grasp of English so as to establish contact with tourists and tourism, learn the most essential aspects of their environment, and are taught a trade. The students are very responsible and are aware that what they are learning will be of great use to them. Furthermore, it has an immediate effect on their work.

The school is set in a leafy garden filled with trees and plants, which sets it apart from the misery that pervades the city on the other side of the wall. It is a privileged space, which was provided by the nuns in the neighbouring convent of Santa Catherine. When the children are enrolled in this school they must take a test to determine their placement. For this reason, there are some quite small children sharing a classroom with much older ones. Before going to class, they line up in perfect rows in the yard, all well combed, to sing the Indian national anthem and say their prayers. From the youngest to the eldest they maintain a strict discipline and carry out everything with great solemnity. But then when they break out of the ranks they become a crowd of children, milling around, noisy, laughing, jumping and pushing their way to their classrooms.

The children come to school very motivated, they are all eyes and ears open to the world. But this idyllic view fades as we become sharply aware of how the teachers must go about their work with a severe shortage of materials. There is no money and any initiative requires a great deal of determination to be brought to fruition. The staff is disenchanted; they are tired of struggling.

My calling to become a teacher came a long time ago, when I was very young. I attended the Santa Anna School in Barcelona and all the pupils took an active part in the education process. At midday I would stay for lunch and the responsibility I enjoyed most of all was taking care of the younger ones, telling them stories and putting them to sleep. I always knew that I wanted to be a teacher. Once I was grown up, aside from having a good time with the kids, enriching myself every day, and coming home with new experiences from which I drew the vitality to keep me on my toes, I was able to identify the real motives that made me want to join this profession: it seems to sum up all that I have been given by those around me. If I am the outcome of my parents' dedication, of the teaching I have received, of the support I had of those who were at my side, then I cannot keep this good fortune to myself. I have to pass it on, to become a part of the wheel of continuous exchange by taking on the role of an educator.

The moment arrives to take the plunge and get to work with the kids of the Andheri quarter. Noel, the director, takes me on a guided tour of the whole school and leaves me with the class that I am going to teach English. My English is not fluent enough to give lessons, but I am not about to give up so I do a version of the song *En Joan petit quan balla* (*When Little John dances*, a traditional Catalan children's song that involves naming the different parts of the body) because I know that some days ago they learned the parts of the anatomy. We do all the movements together and it turns out quite well. But my efforts to try to teach a little English to that collection of curious eyes, which don't really understand if I am from over here or over there, are not too successful.

I am full of good intentions and want to get involved as much as possible, but until I decide to go to the carpentry workshop I can't say that I really broke through. Thomas is running the workshop when I charge in and disrupt everything he has planned. With no regard for what he is trying to do, and without a thought for the consequences, I skip the protocol and suggest that the children make a wooden frame for photographs. All well and good. But things are not that simple. Everything has to be made by hand and there are almost no tools. With the few resources we have and a good dose of imagination, the frames finally start to take shape. The result is very satisfying. At the school where I work in Barcelona, we are surrounded by facilities that we never really appreciate; the kids don't realise how much they have available to them. But for these kids, every tiny detail is a victory worth celebrating. This makes me feel like I definitely want to stay on now.

As far as languages are concerned, I always took it as given that if you had ever spoken a language once, especially as a child, you could never really lose it. That's why I thought that when I heard Marathi spoken again I would recognise words, phrases... who knows, I might even be able to speak it. But things did not live up to my expectations. What a disappointment! JNN had one set of classes in Hindi and another in Marathi, the language I am told I spoke when I was at the orphanage, the language I must have thought in when I arrived in Barcelona. The fact is that I don't understand a word of either language. I go along to the Marathi classes but no matter how hard I try to recover that lost portion of my memory, nothing happens. I don't recognise any of it. The best thing is probably to treat it as a game, as something new to learn, and so I decide to start from scratch. To begin with, the boys and girls don't understand how I can be Indian like them but don't understand and cannot speak their language. They soon get over that and enjoy teaching me basic vocabulary. One by one they say their names, they teach me the colours, they show me how to say everything in sight: tree, sky, flower, house, book, sun, cloud. Between their scrambled English and my rudimentary Marathi we manage to transform the classroom into bedlam.

Aside from speaking Marathi I must also have learned English at the orphanage. But as I used to play truant to go on my daily jaunts with Mother Adelina, I often skipped the English classes. My parents, who were waiting for me in Barcelona, knew nothing of my early fondness for evading classes, and put all their energy into learning English so they could communicate with me when the time arrived. A few months before my arrival, they hired an English teacher who gave them private lessons at the dining table in their home. These classes were focused specifically on teaching them the most practical things. Mum, always worried, wanted to be able to ask me what kind of things I liked to eat, what kind of pain I was in, and to tell me that she loved me a lot. Both of them studied hard but it was all in vain. When I arrived I found they had decorated the flat for me, and Dad, always the practical one, translated word for word, dictionary in hand, the sign they had made which read, 'WELCOME TO HOME, ASHA'. Excited as I was to suddenly find that I had some new parents, a sister, a home, and a bed of my own, all in the same day, I didn't pay much attention to the poster. On the way home from the airport my parents spoke to me in English and I nattered away like a chatterbox in Marathi. Thank goodness for the power of looks, gestures and caresses. I was quite happy to settle for the physical demonstration of their affection. There is always a universal language that cuts across all frontiers, and can establish a form of communication as good as – if not better than – using words from the dictionary. It became pretty clear on the way home that I didn't speak English.

Sunday, 27th October, 1974
Asha, my dear daughter, today you arrived in Barcelona.
We were so nervous that we arrived at the airport long
before we needed to. It was lucky that we did, because the

*plane landed more than half an hour ahead of schedule: at
10:20 exactly.*

*After passing through all the security checks, the two
of us, accompanied by our friend who is an air hostess,
finally arrived at the landing area. When the aircraft came
to a standstill and the stairs had been put in place we stood
there alongside it, waiting to see you come down. It was
a very emotional moment. Once the door was open you
appeared, jumping agilely down the stairs. So tiny. You
came down happy with a big smile stretching from ear to
ear. On reaching the ground you turned and threw yourself
into our arms. You were wonderful. You kissed each of us
and Fatima, and nothing seemed strange to you. In the car,
on the way to what will be your home from now on, you
seemed happy and repeated, in a very sweet manner, all
the words we told you. Dad, Fatima and I watched you
in admiration...*

*You are so happy that all our worries have evaporated. I think
that you like us and that our meeting, which I have imagined
to myself so many times, easily surpassed all my expectations.
What joy!*

*And so you came into the house and took off your
shoes. They must have been new and were probably
uncomfortable. In any case it seemed like you were not
too accustomed to wearing them. With all the changes that
were going on, little Fatima went all quiet. When she saw
you coming down from the plane and how you embraced
us and gave us each a kiss, she didn't know what to do. I
have been talking to her about you for a few days now...*

At first she pulled a face, but her bad mood soon wore off, especially when you, Asha, filled the pockets of her trousers with sweets.

Above all she began to fall in love when you gave her the doll; she clutched it to her and has not let go of it since. I suppose that little by little she will get used to the idea of having a sister. When you and Dad went to fetch your suitcase, Fatima ran along behind calling your name.

In the dining room Dad asked you to read the poster which he had drawn with such care, but you, my darling, just glanced at it and carried on doing your own thing. That is when we realised that you still don't know how to read, which means that we shall have to start from scratch.

The funniest thing about the whole scene was seeing Dad trailing you around with an English dictionary, trying to make himself understood. The more things he asked you, the more excitedly you chatted away in your own language. Finally, he gave up and following more innate instincts he opted for body language and signs.

Sitting in the middle of the dining room you opened your suitcase and handed out presents to everyone. Dad spent a long time immortalising those wonderful moments of happiness by taking photographs and filming.

You look tired and who knows if you managed to sleep or not during the journey. I take you to the bathroom and wash you from top to bottom in the shower. You are very thin; above all it shows in the legs and the arms which look like matchsticks. I am sure you are anaemic and when you see the doctor he will probably prescribe all kinds of vitamins. It is lovely to see how excited you are about every little thing.

After you had had your bath and your pyjamas were on with the dressing gown I made for you, in blue, like your sister Fatima's, you were overcome with joy. You looked at yourself in the mirror over and over, and you jumped and laughed with happiness. What luck that even though we can't understand each other's words we can make ourselves understood through looks, hugs and smiles.

It seems to us that this day marks the end of a very important episode in our lives. It all began with Dad and me, two people who loved one another. And little by little we have started to grow in number. Those little girls who we so much wanted, arrived from far away. First there was a tiny little one and then the big one. So we have managed to hop over the laws of logic and nature all in one go. Being a parent is always a great responsibility, but it is even more so when fate decides to place not one but two little children in your arms, to educate and feed, in body and in spirit. It is in this moment of reflection, of pleasure and also of fear, that you find your father and me, dear Asha.

5

The Spiral Staircase

Today the alarm clock rings before the sound of Naresh's prayer bells. Maria, Nuria and Gabriela are sleeping in, taking advantage of the fact that it is Sunday. So I get up without making any noise and carefully pick my way between their sleeping forms to reach the bathroom. As I step into the shower the aroma of incense has already filled the house. The years and years I have waited for this occasion dictate that I dress up properly. Today, more than ever, I want to look smart. I put on the *salwar kameez* I bought at one of the stalls in the market. It is orange and purple; the colours signify the sacred and the feminine.

After arriving in Bombay I realised that the clothes I had brought with me were not the most suitable in the stifling heat. I felt very hot and decided to dress the way Indian women do – partly because of the weather, but also as a sign of having decided to be like them. When I think of Indian women, I imagine them in those saris in all their bright colours: metres and metres of cloth which they wrap around themselves with a unique skill. But I have the feeling that they would never really look right and would feel too much like being in fancy dress. This is why I opted for the *salwar kameez* which consists of a kind of blouse that reaches down to the knees, loose trousers and a scarf that matches the pattern of one of the other two pieces. The *salwar kameez* doesn't quite have the elegance of a sari, but I feel very comfortable and much cooler. I bought a couple so that I could vary them, I've kept this one for the day when I'd return to my orphanage.

Beneath a sky filled with clouds I walk along streets that already feel familiar. I recognise the faces behind the stall selling roasted corn, and the one with baskets of fruit, one with glimmering saris fluttering about, another with spices that give off a blend of perfumes mixed with the strong smell of bidis. At the end of the street I approach the first driver in the row of taxis and, without hesitating, let fly with the address I have been repeating all the way so as to remember it, like a little child running an errand. In reply, I receive a hail of words that I don't understand, but the tone suggests a definite negative. Inside the next taxi I find a guy with his hair dyed a deep red colour who offers to take me.

The journey seems interminable. Mother Adelina told me she would be waiting. A few days ago, when I had been here exactly a week, I called to tell them about my visit. When I identified myself she didn't remember, and it took a long time for her to realise who I was. I imagined she must be very old now and that her memory was failing. When she did finally remember me, she became very excited and insisted that I pay her a visit. Speaking to her on the telephone was a very intense moment. Another step closer to my origins. We talked in Spanish. Mother Adelina is from Puerto Rico and although she has lived in Bombay for so many years she still hasn't lost the language.

Passing through the streets and alleys makes me think of Dad, who knows this city by heart, even though he has never been here. I can see him with that heap of maps laid out on the dining room table, tracing the streets and squares of my city. When my parents decided to adopt me, Dad amused himself for hours with a map of Bombay in front of him looking for the place where I lived, imagining where I walked. He wanted to know what my surroundings were like in order to feel closer to me. Meanwhile, on the other side of the table, Mum would be going through the adoption papers one more time.

The taxi pulls up in front of the impressive wrought iron gate. This image has remained alive in my mind for all these years. To the right of the gate is a nameplate. I don't need to take a closer look to see what is written there, I know perfectly well: Regina Pacis. Suddenly, I am seized by an anxious feeling that freezes my blood. I no longer feel the stifling heat. A tremor runs through me, preventing me from taking the next step, until I remind myself that I am here to reconcile with the past.

❃

The orphanage is like a fortress in which my secret is guarded. I am the only one who can find the key to unlock it. I take a photograph of the gate before I enter the lush garden, full of trees and plants. I slowly follow the path that leads up to the entrance, looking around at everything with emotions that are difficult to describe. The sound of the pebbles I walk over on the path, the little yard on one side where I once played with other children... I can't stop taking pictures, of everything, each and every little detail. I want everything to be properly recorded because I don't want there to be any shadows or blurred images in my memory, and I also need them to help explain my experience when I return to Barcelona.

Everything is as it was twenty years ago. The school is to the right, a conventional looking building, a greyish colour, three floors, no balconies but with wide windows. To the left is a colonial style building, the convent. I take the four steps leading up to the convent entrance hall in one go. In English, I ask the first young nun I see for Mother Adelina. I am a bundle of nerves. She asks me to take a seat on a chair in the hall. My eyes dart from one door to the other as I wonder which one will reveal the nun who was like a mother to me. I look in front of me and recognise the passageway that leads to where the girls live, the place that was home to me from age three to six.

It wasn't easy being just one out of two hundred girls. The rules were very strict and they weren't shy about giving us the occasional slap. The great affection I received from the Nasik nuns until I was three vanished when I arrived here. Although, almost immediately, I became the spoilt little girl, the nuns' favourite.

✥

I don't know how I managed it. Looking back over the years, I clearly recall how life among those girls was ruled by the survival of the fittest; the most alert were the best equipped to survive. I was always covered in scratches and my face was marked by the constant fights: no, it wasn't survival of the fittest, it was the law of the jungle. I was not aware of what I was doing, but I had the fortune of falling into the nuns' good graces. Whenever I could, I would evade my duties and go running to hide in their skirts. I was their little pet.

Regina Pacis was divided into two parts: the school and the orphanage. In the school were girls who came from wealthy families. They were boarders who lived in twin bedrooms, with their own beds, cupboards and bedside tables. We orphans often managed to sneak in and poke our noses into all their things and spy on them. We didn't have rooms of our own. I recall an enormous hall with arches in the ceiling and overhead fans. We each slept on a towel on the floor, all lined up in a row, one next to the other. India is a hot and humid country, and this was reflected in the hall's warm air and the cold, damp floor on which we slept. There was nothing more than a thin towel between the ground and our bodies. A warm country? Perhaps, but we felt cold. The only heat came from the body alongside you. And though we slept closely together I remember feeling lonely. A lot of company, but at the same time very much alone.

The fans went on turning, stirring the air in the hall, but I lacked the air I needed to feel alive. Time went by and each day was an exact copy of the day before, nothing ever changed.

On either side of the living area there was a door which squeaked and allowed no more than a sliver of light through. At night, the slightest sound would wake me up. I would hear those hair raising squeaks and was so scared that I didn't dare budge, not even to go to the toilet. I looked for the little sliver of light, but I was enveloped in fathomless darkness. Each morning there would be the same drama: who wet the bed? Asha. Ever since then I have been easily frightened. The toilets were just alongside that area; a hole in the ground, dirty and disgusting. There was also a dressing room, a row of shelves with a little niche for each of us to leave our clothes in, all our belongings. In contrast to the bare simplicity of all this, the only luxury was a small room for anyone who was ill. It had a bed, which made all the difference.

We got up early and carried our towels out into the yard to air them. Since I often wet myself, time after time I had to hang mine out to let it dry and each day I received a smack for this. But afterwards it was all forgotten and I would go and play with the nuns. When the towels were put away the hall was free to be used for other activities. On one occasion, when we were supposed to have been at risk from I don't know what infection, the nuns prepared a large pot filled with a liquid of indeterminate colour and we had to pass by in single file to be given a couple of spoonfuls each. Such an awful taste! That scene remains forever etched in my mind. The rich girls in the boarding school used to receive visits every weekend from their parents. We girls in the orphanage had been abandoned for reasons we did not know and would not have understood then. We watched those meetings from the other side of the fence while parents smiled and gave presents to their daughters. They would embrace them, their eyes shining with happiness. I had the affection of the nuns, all of them would make a fuss over me, but it wasn't the same. I might not have needed the parents, but I did want the happiness. And so one fine day, when I was five years old, I crossed the passage that connected us to the nuns' residence. They were praying on the upper floor. I didn't hesitate for a second. I went up the spiral staircase made of wood and sat down in the last row until they finished their prayers. It was an old wooden staircase and each step creaked as I trod on it. When Mother Adelina came out of the oratory I said to her, 'I want some parents!' That ascending spiral became transformed in my mind into a symbol of my quest, and for an entire year I climbed that staircase every day to sit on the top step and ask her if she had found any yet. Poor woman, what could she say to that little creature asking for so much?

At that time and in that place, adoptions were not very common. The religious community took charge of teaching the girls, and as they got older they ensured that they had enough for a dowry and a husband. The option of not wanting to get married did not exist, unless of course a girl should decide she wanted to become a nun. From a very tender age a path was marked out for their futures, without their having any say in the matter, without the power to make decisions about their own lives. At times I was seized by negative feelings towards those nuns who scolded me the most. I always thought that one day, when I was grown, I would come back to show them how I had turned out. I only wanted them to understand how I felt.

When it was time to go to school I tried to get out of it as much as I could. I would run up and down barefoot chasing the nuns all day. Perhaps I was such a prankster because some kind of intuition told me that my life would not end there, that one day my life would be free. Thanks to my obstinacy I was given the opportunity to see a bit of the world, which meant a few walks through Bombay. Mother Adelina was in charge of relations with the outside community and she took me along whenever she could. The other girls never left the compound, but I did. After questioning her daily at the top of the staircase, Mother Adelina would give me an apple and we would cross the garden and go through the gate to find a taxi. We would visit all of the city's grand hotels, such as the Taj Mahal, where we collected extra food to bring back to the orphanage. We orphans, of course, wouldn't see a morsel of it. We were given nothing more than rice and vegetables, no fish or meat. All of those succulent treats must have wound up on the plates of the rich girls.

In response to my demands for a family, Mother Adelina would always say that I had to pray more and have faith. Without saying a word, however, she wrote a letter in Spanish explaining my case and put my photograph in the envelope. That letter travelled, via an intermediary in Barcelona, thousands of kilometres from Bombay to the house of Josep Miró and Electa Vega, who never thought that one day they would wind up as my parents. They were engaged in trying to adopt a pair of Indian twins. Because they were so deeply immersed in the whole business, it was hoped that they might be able to find a family for this other child who was a little older. The twins were Fatima and Mary. They were born in Gujurat, in the north of India. Their parents were as young as they were poor and couldn't take responsibility for them. The same religious order of Regina Pacis has a centre in Gujurat and that is where they were taken in for little more than a year. My parents were very excited about adopting twins. That way, they could give two children a new life, with the same amount of effort. A few days before the plane was due to take them to Barcelona, they were transferred to the orphanage in Bombay. Mary fell ill. She caught a simple case of measles, which she would have recovered from at home with a few days in bed and the right medication. But she didn't make it. Mary's death led to the start of my second life. Mary, Fatima and I lived under the same roof, unaware that destiny would bring us together.

Once they managed to get over this situation, our parents decided that Fatima should have a sister anyway, and they applied to adopt another baby. Meanwhile, the letter with my photo was lying on the sideboard in their dining room. Each time they lifted it up to dust they would promise themselves to try to find me some parents, until one day a light went on in Mum's head and she decided it would be better to adopt a child than a newborn, so they applied for me. When Mary died, I was six, almost seven years old. And while I knew nothing of the matter, everything went ahead until all that remained were the formalities of the adoption. Mother Adelina had her work cut out convincing the other nuns of the benefits of an adoption. They'd had no warning and were not familiar with the process. It wasn't usually an option in their educational programme, and I suppose that they cared for me. But they had to concede and finally, one morning, so early that the time for the daily ritual of climbing the spiral staircase had not even arrived, Mother Adelina came to tell me the news: 'You've got some parents!' She gave me a black-and-white photograph. From that moment on, I carried the photo of the people who were to be my parents in my pocket everywhere I went. To me, they were already my parents, and the picture became creased and worn from all the time I spent looking at and kissing it. Fatima was also in the photo. I had a little sister. That was an extra gift that I hadn't even dreamed of. I clearly recall many of the moments I spent with that photo in my pocket and the happiness I felt knowing that I would have a family, just like those other girls I had spied on.

The months of preparation to join my new family were an adventure full of emotions. Mother Adelina and I took advantage of our tours around the hotels of Bombay by taxi. One day we would go shopping for warm clothes – I would need a coat in Barcelona. Another day for shoes – I had never had any before – and a suitcase, bigger than me, to put it all in. She advised me on all the purchases we made but let me choose the colour of the coat, the skirts, the kind of shoes I wanted and above all, what kind of presents I wanted to take with me. She made me feel like a big girl. We went to the souvenir shops where I bought a colourful picture made of wood for Dad; for Mum, some paper dancers that moved when you touched them, and for Fatima, a doll, a game with little animals and a sari. Something for everyone, and the suitcase was growing fuller each day. Of the clothes that I had in my niche, I kept nothing, I left it all behind. I imagined that it would be passed on to the next girl, the one who would occupy my towel, my niche, and who, most probably, would not be as lucky as I was. It was the end of that period of my life, everything had to be new for my new life ahead.

A sound from the hall brings me back to the present. One of the doors I have been watching has opened and slowly the blurred image I have of Mother Adelina takes form. An elderly woman appears, about eighty years old, thin and small, with white skin and dressed all in white. My eyes mist up at the sight of her, and I shed all the tears that have been building up inside me since I came back to my country. We embrace and I feel as though nothing has changed, only that we are both much older. We sit down in the hall to talk but immediately are joined by the other nuns. Some of them are old dears like Adelina, but there are younger ones too. They surround me and in no time it becomes a cat's chorus of wailing voices: Don't you remember me? I washed your hair. I dressed you. I took you to class... I didn't remember any of the others. In the midst of this uproar, a mixture of Spanish and English, Mother Adelina and I exchanged a look which felt very familiar.

They told me that when I went to them to ask for breakfast I always used to say: 'It's time to ten'. Since I was always playing truant, my English was a little precarious. It seems that the expression, which is quite meaningless, caught on and that even today there is always someone who says, 'It's time to ten'. The younger nuns offer to show me around the school facilities and the orphanage. Nothing has changed. Right in the middle of the courtyard, where on Saturdays we used to take turns riding a bicycle and on Sundays we would lie in the sun, there was still a big rusty barrel filled with water. How many times had I drunk from there! In the branches of a tree a crow seemed to be watching me. I lead the nuns over to the other side to get away from it. Crows always make me panic. When I was small, in this same courtyard, a crow once tore at my hair and scratched my neck. My impressions and foggy memories of my childhood now appear to me as real episodes. Behind the house I find the same big basins for washing clothes. The nuns come with me to the workshops where they teach dressmaking, cooking and dancing. Then, out of the corner of my eye, I spot it: the spiral staircase, the most vivid symbol of my path; it exists, and is not the fruit of some distorted memory. I can't really take it all in. There are too many images at once, but inside me certain pieces that were dislocated are beginning to find their place. The girls who live here now have prepared a song for me. They show me their drawings. In the middle of all the excitement I see in their eyes a trace of unhappiness mixed with the admiration they feel towards me. The emotions are overwhelming.

It is lunch time. The same rice and vegetables they served twenty years ago and a cake, which they have baked in celebration of my visit. The nuns talk about today in comparison to what it was like in my day. They talk about the differences, how everything has changed and how adoption has become a regular occurrence. Every year there are girls who leave this orphanage to go to families that will take care of them, either in this country or further afield. They tell me about the problems they have with the new generations of girls, both in school and in the orphanage. For my part, I tell them about the two purposes of my visit: to rediscover my past, and to take part in the Setem work camps. We could have carried on chatting for hours, but as in any hot country, there is one sacred ritual: the afternoon siesta.

By now I really feel like spending some time alone with Mother Adelina, and she feels the same. Finally we have a moment to ourselves, to catch up on what has happened in our lives. She grips my arm – leaning on me – and we withdraw. Her health is quite delicate, her memory is going and the slightest movement requires a great effort. We walk slowly along the passageways to her room. Going inside is, for me, like stepping over the threshold of a temple. Only these walls know how much hard work she put into giving me an opportunity. Her eyes reflect the joy she feels at seeing me, knowing that it was worth the effort to try to find me a family, give me a new start in life. Mother Adelina observes me carefully; she hasn't stopped watching me since I arrived. But now that the two of us are alone it is as if she is suddenly aware of the twenty years during which she has not seen me, as if by looking at me she might be able to confirm that she did the right thing by sending that letter with my photo inside. I imagine she is as moved as I am, if not more so. I also imagine that she realises I am happy and that the parents I asked her for, the parents I found in Barcelona, have turned me into a well educated and happy woman.

The sun is going down and the little strands of light that filter through the lowered blinds give this humble room a tint of gold, as though it were filled with the most precious treasure. A bed, a table and a chair. On top of the table are lots of boxes, each with a name, one box for each of her girls now distributed around the world. They are made of tin, like the kind you put biscuits in. With trembling hands she finds mine and Fatima's and pulls out a yellow envelope from inside. It is full of photos from when we were small. The most worn of all is the first picture my parents sent me at the orphanage. On the back I recognise Mum's writing: 'These are your parents and your little sister, who are waiting for you.'

Tied together with a piece of string are all the letters I wrote to the home over the last two decades. Mum started it, writing to tell them about our progress and what our life was like in Barcelona. Fatima and I took it up from there, telling stories about school, an excursion or the grades we were getting. I enjoyed telling them about the progress I was making on the piano. Going through the letters I come across Fatima's drawing of the pool where we learned to swim.

As I get older the letters maintain the same structure. At certain times in my life, during adolescence above all, I needed someone to confide in. There were a lot of things which I couldn't really talk about to those who were closest to me. Mother Adelina would have been the perfect person; she knew me better than anyone and, furthermore, now I had even learned to speak her language! But I was never able to establish that close personal contact with her, because all the letters were written when we were all together. I would have liked to let it all out, tell her about the first boy I liked; that suffering which makes you feel you are dying. I also needed someone to talk to about how overprotective my parents could be. They didn't want anything in our surroundings to hurt me, and at times this was suffocating. Of course, now that I am older, I understand what my parents wanted for me and I am infinitely indebted to them.

I tie the letters back together and start pestering her with all the questions to which I still have not found any answers. After twenty years I am finally certain that my vague memories, those faded images, correspond to something real. She tells me all about the day that I left. I said my farewells to everyone without any sign of sadness, calmly. I walked towards happiness with such determination that she felt it wasn't normal in such a small girl. At the airport, once I had passed through the glass door I waved goodbye without shedding a single tear. Now that I am grown I often wish I had the same strength I had then.

Mother Adelina continues her story with plenty of other anecdotes about my stay here, but she manages to evade one wound that remains very much open. She tells me that when I was three years old the nuns in Nasik decided to send me to Bombay because I would be able to go to school there, but she doesn't give me any further details. She knows where I come from but she won't give me the information, she wants to spare me the suffering and thinks that she is protecting me. After a lot of circling around I start to become more insistent. I want her to clear up the doubts that have led me back here. I want to know who my real biological parents are, why they abandoned me, why they didn't love me, what kind of situation they were in that I was such a burden they had to get rid of. It is very painful that so many years have gone by without answers. Mother Adelina tells me not to stir up the past, that I should look ahead, the past can only do me harm, that I have the best life I could possibly imagine and that I should give thanks to God for this gift, for all the love my family has given me, for not having to suffer the poverty that afflicts India. And she adds: 'It shouldn't matter to you whether you are the child of rich or poor people, the sacred waters of India gave you life and the only thing you have to think about is to live the gift of God with dignity, helping others, doing good.'

'Don't stop me,' I insist. 'I want to know more, I need it.'

To silence me she says: 'Asha, you are a daughter of the Ganges.'

The moment finally arrives when it is time for me to leave. We make a symbolic exchange before we part: I swap my Panama Jack sandals, strong and supportive, for hers, which are almost falling to pieces and hurt her tired, sensitive feet. She gave me the wings to fly. In some way I give her the shoes so that she can carry on along the path that still remains for her. Finally, we hug each other emotionally. I squeeze her so tightly that I make her stagger. Poor dear! She is so frail. I squeeze her with all the affection I feel for one of the most important people in my life. I turn to cross the garden towards the wrought iron gate and I begin to see that the memories are starting to settle into place. But I still leave with a slightly bitter taste: there is one piece missing. I did not manage to complete the puzzle of my life that would allow me to fully face the future. I stop once more to look at the orphanage from outside before taking a taxi to the house of Naresh and Kamal. I feel lighter than I did a few hours ago.

Monday, 28th October, 1974
Today, at seven in the morning, you woke up, Asha, completely terrified. Your cry of 'Mummy, Mummy' gave me a start and I came running to your room. You

looked like you had had a nightmare, my poor girl. We have the problem of the language, but with gestures you made me understand that you were afraid of the dark and you wanted the light on. I feel so bad that we can't communicate verbally... You would have been able to tell me that you were afraid, that you had dreams that scared you so much... I would love to be able to comfort you and tell you that there is nothing for you to worry about here, that you are with us and we will not allow anything bad to happen to you. I gave you a tight hug and you understood that. On the lower bunk your sister Fatima had also woken up. Because it was still early I carried both of you to our bed and there all four of us had a lot of fun. You and Fatima played trying to tickle each other and your father and I felt incredibly happy. Your father is completely mad about taking photographs of these precious moments. He went to fetch his camera, and with the automatic setting we took photos of all four of us together. I am bursting with joy. I know there are feelings that neither photos nor these badly written words can manage to describe, but I shall settle for leaving this account and perhaps one day, when you become a mother, you will understand each and every one of these emotions.

After all of this uproar, the day to day activities began, for you as well as for us. We went out to buy clothes and shoes.

The nuns had bought you most of the essentials for the journey but the clothes you brought are too thin for the cold weather that is just beginning in Barcelona.

How lovely it is to go out in the street with my little girls. In the neighbourhood, everyone stops us to say hello. You add a touch of colour. Some of them mutter 'poor things', and you can't imagine how much this bothers me; others might think I must have lost my marbles to embark on this adventure. But they don't know, my girl, that for us it is not an adventure, it is our life.

At the shoeshop I had a battle on my hands to get you to try on some school shoes. There was no way of persuading you. You picked out some other shoes, very elegant, but not practical for playing in the schoolyard. I don't know how I managed to get you to understand, but in the end you went along with me.

The next episode was at the butcher's. You looked at the meat and started stamping your feet on the ground and shaking your head. It is at moments like this that I wish you could speak. I imagine that you have never eaten meat in your life.

Your father and I have read a lot of books about the customs in your country. It helped us to feel a little closer to you while we were going through with the adoption. We had books and maps scattered all over the dining room table. Your father looked at the map of Bombay, locating where the orphanage was, the Spanish embassy, the courts, the famous Victoria Station, the Taj Mahal Hotel. Each day he would take a different route, imagining which way you would have to go to get to the airport. Sometimes I feel sorry I missed the early years of your infancy, the moments when you were discovering the world around you. I envy the people who were at your side and took care of you, but now I have you here, and with all the time in the world ahead of us.

Lunch time has been a bit of a struggle. You turn your nose up at everything. I know it is difficult for you but you will have to get used to our eating habits. To avoid eating you burst into tears with sobs that would break anyone's heart. I have no choice but to force you a little, because you are very undernourished and you must have a terrible case of anaemia.

What makes me marvel is that I thought it would be more difficult with a girl who was a little older. I thought that perhaps I wouldn't be able to manage, that you would have problems adapting. But right now everything is going as smooth as silk, and I hope and pray that this feeling of harmony is mutual.

6

Something to Offer

rriving in Bombay, the group from Barcelona divided into two: those of us who would work as volunteers in the school, and those who would work in a refuge for women in a run down area. There is a lot of prostitution in that zone and all the problems of destitution associated with it. It is a very sordid area, an extensive shanty town constructed with the worst materials – plastic, cardboard – and the sanitary conditions are horrendous. It is a feat to just get hold of clean drinking water. The women who prostitute themselves live in these tiny rooms with their children. Those infants have to leave the shack when their mother needs to work and they run aimlessly through the alleyways which hold no possibility of escape, or else they are made to hide under the bed and try to sleep because they have learned that they are not to be any trouble. Their reward is not a doll or a bicycle, but a handful of rice or lentils.

The group that works there is demoralised. They feel useless because even a small change in an environment as run down as this will begin to become apparent only in the very long term. Westerners always feel a need to achieve results quickly. Perplexity and impotence make you want to turn the whole thing upside down, but effective help can come only with a profound understanding of the culture, traditions, and spirituality which motivates people. The moment to actually do something comes only after having learned to listen.

The project set up in this neighbourhood is a refuge for women and their children. They are given food to combat nutrition deficiencies and an attempt is made to teach them a trade that will help them get ahead. The project also campaigns to teach people about AIDS and other illnesses. Supplying these essentials demands a great deal of compassion, in addition to water, rice and medicine.

Those of us working at the school go to the women's cooperative some afternoons to lend a hand. We receive widows and women rejected by their husbands. Some of them have suffered abuse or apparent accidents, which are really intentional acts of aggression, such as the disfigurement of their faces with acid. They are women whom society has turned its back on. They have been led to believe that they are worthless and will never improve their lives. But this cooperative, which started from nothing, has continued to grow among the locals. There are more women all the time who are capable of doing work that affords them a decent life. They live in shared houses and do manual work, mostly with textiles. The range of products has also grown: rag dolls, bags, aprons, towels, coverlets, cushions... all decorated with traditional patterns as well as declarations on women's rights. These objects are sold in Europe through organisations dedicated to fair trade, which guarantees that the people are fairly paid. With this work they are able to recover their personal dignity and life begins to make sense again. Some of those who have been attacked with acid are able to travel to Europe for operations, which opens up a new life for them.

❦

Those of us who travel to India with their heads full of good intentions and a will to work and make themselves useful, often find themselves disillusioned because a month is barely long enough to find your feet and make a difference. Yet in retrospect I realise that these work camps are focused primarily on having us observe and learn from everything around us. All the things we have experienced will continue to grow inside us and once we return home we won't just throw ourselves down on the sofa and watch the world pass us by, but rather get to work and try to change things as best we can.

I came back to India to do something useful and so I spend hours at the school in the neighbourhood of Andheri instead of simply being a tourist. I want to return to Barcelona with something to show for it, to have contributed in some way. I know that the work camps thrust me directly into the toughest side of the country and that India is more than destitution, children forced to work and women who have been abused. I spent years learning about my country from books and documentries. I know that it is a country rich in many things. A country where people of different religions, more than thirty official languages and an infinity of dialects, are able to live together in varying degrees of harmony. India is a country with a culture that stretches back thousands of years, and that can be felt on the streets of this city. Bombay is also host to the Indian cinema industry, so impressive as to be dubbed 'Bollywood'. India is an overpopulated country filled with contrasts that reach astonishing extremes. These days, between trying to fit into the daily lives of the children at school, and my own interior journey of returning to the country where I was born, I continue to wonder what my life would have been like if I had not been adopted. It is like a personal riddle and I still have no answer.

It will not be long before I shall go to Nasik with the rest of the group, and I feel a bundle of nerves in my stomach. I will have two tasks there: to learn about the water conservation project, and to dig into the most remote parts of my personal history. I hope to meet someone who still retains some memory of me, that the monsoons have not washed it all away.

Tuesday, 29th October, 1974

I couldn't sleep in the early hours of this morning and I came in to see you in your room. Both of my little darlings in a deep, calm sleep. Like all mothers, I watch over you night and day. During the day I see in your eyes a joy which is contagious, at night I hear your steady breathing, like the rolling of the waves. It is marvellous to be your mother.

These days, Asha, the simple dialogue of signs and hugs is helping us to get along. Your laughter is only silenced during meal times. Every day we have a little quarrel, but your tears are not going to make me give up. My dear girl, if you don't eat, you won't grow. Perhaps I should devote more time to you, but Fatima has been jealous ever since you arrived and also demands my attention. Aside from that, I can see she is quite happy for you to follow after her all day, playing and leading her around. You spin her round and play all kinds of tricks on her, and when you finally set her down she staggers about until she can get her balance. She is not as advanced as she ought to be and has only just learned to walk, yet you make her rush around like a rocket.

Your arrival has required great changes. When we started thinking about adoption, I decided that I would have to give up my job to devote all my time to the two of you. But you pay me back in all manner of ways. I can say that I am better off now than I was before. From this point on I shall have time to sew for my little girls and take part in all your little discoveries.

7

Mary

Wednesday, 30th October, 1974
Dearest Asha, you don't really leave me much time to write these days but I want to tell you my story. When I got married I wanted to have a family, and I imagined what it would be like. I always said to your father that I should like to have twins. It was a dream and as the years went by it stayed like that, just a dream. Health problems meant that I had to have surgery a number of times... and without what nature provides for procreation, you can ask for the moon but it won't make a difference. Fate made reality of an impossibility. We were to adopt two babies;

Fatima and Mary. They were not the fruit of my womb, but of my most intimate wishes.

A few months ago Mary closed her eyes, unable to beat the illness she was fighting. And so fate took away what it had given me. And it is thanks to all of these twists and turns that you are here with us.

One day, leafing through a book, your father came across an anonymous poem in which all of your names appear. Yes, the names of all three of my daughters: Asha, Fatima and Mary (Marien):

'Tres morillas me enamoran en Jaén
Asha, Fatima y Marien'★

Just like the poet, I am also in love with my three girls... You are the most important thing I have! Now you see that you must keep on believing in your dreams and one day, sooner or later, they will all come true.

Every new day is special, as much for the intensity of our lives in the different volunteer camps and our coexistence with the people of this country, as for all the turmoil I feel from confronting my history. Once I have showered and dressed, Kamal leads me by the arm and makes me sit on the carpet that covers the living room floor. She is proud that I am dressing as an Indian and she wants to add her

★'I fell in love with three Moorish maids in Jaén; Asha, Fatima and Marien.'

personal touch. Each morning she does my hair in a different way. One braid or two, or a whole bunch of them plaited together. All day long she is rushing around, seeing to the children and the housework, but she has transformed the act of doing my hair into a ritual. She brushes the hair energetically but unhurriedly and separates the strands to braid them. It has been years since anyone brushed my hair and the feeling is so pleasant that I shut my eyes and let myself go. These are perhaps the only moments when I can let my mind go blank, no thoughts... I spend too much time worrying. Today is going to be particularly trying. She knows where I am going and I interpret her efforts to make today's braiding more intricate than usual as a way of saying she will be there with me. She stands in the doorway to wave goodbye as I walk up the street. I stop to buy some flowers. I skip over a couple of puddles left by the last downpour and carry on to the taxi rank. Again I recite the address which my father once circled on his map of Bombay. I have another appointment with Mother Adelina. First we are going to Mass and afterwards to the cemetery.

It is an unavoidable duty, but I am doing it as much for myself as for my parents and Fatima. After bombarding me with questions about what I was going to do, Mum said quietly, 'Asha, make sure you go and visit your sister, little Mary's grave.'

The flowers I have bought are for Mary. I can't avoid thinking that she would be twenty-two years old now, like Fatima. And what would have become of me? Would I have stayed in India forever? Would I ever have been adopted? By the same parents? We would have been three sisters then, what a handful that would have been. Poor Mum!

In front of Mary's grave, Mother Adelina takes my hands in hers, which are trembling, and she tells me that they did everything they could for her. We sit on a bench facing it and think a while in silence. I stifle my tears in front of Mother Adelina and say a prayer to my parents' daughter, Fatima's twin and, now more than ever, my sister. Mother Adelina prays with me, silently. Mum and Dad would so much have wished to be here.

While I divide the flowers into two bunches to place one on either side of the memorial stone, Mother Adelina tells me that on the day of Mary's funeral, when the ceremony was over and they had gone back to the convent, they received a call from Barcelona. Mum, worried, was asking if the little girl was all right. It was the middle of the night in Barcelona and Mum had been woken up by a nightmare. She had heard a baby crying in pain. Anxiously, she called Bombay and they had to tell her that Mary had fallen ill at the last moment and that she had died.

The nuns put up a memorial stone with words in English in the name of those parents who had already adopted her.

DARLING BABY MARY YOU WENT TO HEAVEN
JUST BEFORE YOU COULD COME TO LIVE WITH US
BUT DEEP IN OUR HEARTS YOU WILL ALWAYS STAY
AS OUR DEAR DAUGHTER
YOUR LOVING FOSTER PARENTS
JOSEP CATALÁ MIRÓ AND ELECTA VEGA DE MIRÓ
BARCELONA, SPAIN
BORN NOV. 2TH 1972 EXPIRED MAY 31ST 1974

During the time when Fatima and Mary where staying at the orphanage in Bombay, I was already making a nuisance of myself asking for a set of parents. And Mother Adelina said that sometimes, at the top of the spiral staircase, I would ask for parents from Barcelona. What could I have known of Barcelona? In all my nosing around I must have picked up on the fact that two girls were about to be adopted by a family in Barcelona. That's the only explanation I can think of. That exotic name must have sounded like the promised land. I imagine that in my subconscious I must have associated that city with an equation for happiness: Barcelona = Happiness = Parents.

For Mother Adelina, today's trip to the cemetery, with all the memories it has stirred up, has been very exhausting. In response to some of my questions she seems brusque and evasive. I don't want to upset her any further. I am not dispirited though. I still have to go to Nasik, where I hope to find out more about my past. I accompany her to the convent and, once again, turn to say goodbye. I have the premonition this will really be the last goodbye and that I shall never see her again. She tells me that she will always be by my side, as she has been all these years, and I believe her. We embrace one last time in front of the wrought iron gate and I remain there, but I'm not sure why. I could have walked up with her, arm in arm, to the house. But I stay there, watching her advance slowly, wearing my sandals, through the garden until she turns and waves goodbye with a smile before going inside.

Friday, 1ˢᵗ November, 1974
The last few days have been turned upside down by our visits to the doctor. As we did with your sister, we asked them to give you a complete check up. And, just as in the case of Fatima, the doctor was alarmed to see what sort of a state you were in. He repeated almost word for word the same thing: 'This girl is not the weight nor the height she ought to be for someone of her age. She also has a considerable case of anaemia, and in these circumstances it is difficult to be sure that she will grow normally and that other aspects of her development will not be affected...' My girl, the truth is that you really are skinny... you weigh sixteen kilos and you are one metre twelve in height. I was alarmed about Fatima because all the doctors came to the conclusion that she would not make it... I would like them

to see her now that she has learned to walk. This is why I am not too worried about you; I feel sure that you will recover very soon.

Tomorrow is Fatima's birthday. It will be an important moment for all of us. It is her first birthday at home. Up until now we have simply celebrated our 'first moments'. With you we have had your first day at home, first bath, first night, first tears. Tomorrow we shall celebrate your sister's second birthday. It is now almost six months since she arrived and it seems to have gone by very quickly. Everything is so intense!..

I am sorry I don't know more about your former lives; I know so little that I feel embarrassed when we visit the doctor. They ask me questions about you which I can't answer. When you are grown up the two of you will also ask me questions and I won't be able to answer you either. I am giving you this account so that the small details I write down can help to make up for the time that we have been separated. As a mother, I suppose the fact of knowing your children's past puts your mind at rest to some extent when facing the future.

8

The Rear Entrance

There are no classes today at Andheri. The schoolyard has been decorated with flowers and banners to celebrate India's day of independence. For days the boys and girls, with the help of the teachers and the volunteers, have been busy preparing their activities for today. First, the children sing the national anthem, just as they do every day, but with more intensity. Then there are the dances, and the oldest ones perform a piece of theatre recreating the most important moment in the life of Gandhi. The smaller children look on entranced, their eyes wide with amazement.

When they start to hand out the drinks and the sweets, Nuria, Gabriela and I greet the teachers and the headmaster with a traditional *namaste*. It is a simple gesture, heavy with significance. With the hands brought together as though in prayer, you give yourself to the other person in all humility.

We take advantage of our day off to finally do some sightseeing. We take the train from Andheri station to the Gate of India. If the buses are normally packed, the trains are so full you can't get in edgewise. The wagons are crammed with people pushing and shoving, stuffed with bundles and packages, and with people hanging off the front, shouting at every stop. A little squashed, we manage, nevertheless, to arrive at the legendary Gate of India which dominates the port of Bombay. In the harbour, the dirty grey turbulent sea rises into a mass of heavy clouds about to burst. Plastic kites provide little dots of colour. Everyone, from the children to the old people, is busy flying them higher and higher. There are so many that we remain there, mesmerised by the endless swirls they carve in the sky. All three of us end up with cricks in our necks from looking upwards for so long.

After standing for a good while in a queue as chaotic as the traffic in the port, we board a boat to take us to Elephant Island. During the crossing, the breeze does not manage to alleviate the stifling humidity that makes my trousers stick to my thighs and to the wooden seat. I have the feeling we haven't chosen the best day to go on a tourist trip. It would be worthwhile buying a postcard because the photos are all going to have the grey background of the sea and the sky, and with the boat tossing so much none of them are going to be in focus.

On top of everything else, it starts to rain in earnest. We disembark after an hour and take refuge in the caves on the island. It was the Portuguese who named the island after the huge sculpture that awaits you when you disembark. Naturally, it represents an elephant. The island's main attraction is the four temples cut into the rock. There are reliefs on the walls of the caves where you can make out the outlines of divinities including Shiva, Parvati and Ganesh. We walk along following the images, marvelling at the beauty hidden within the stone.

It has stopped raining and a pallid sun allows us to see an island luxuriant in every shade of green. Avoiding the temptation of the stalls selling necklaces and shells, we return to the boat, but as we are waiting I still manage to fall for some stone elephant souvenirs. Each elephant contains another, smaller elephant inside it, as a symbol of fertility.

⁂

After lunch we lose ourselves in the streets and alleys. I watch the people pass us by. The streets are full of enormous film posters which I now realise are hand painted. The men, standing high up on scaffolds, work with careful brushstrokes. This image, and that of the women who work as building labourers, pushing bricks in a wheelbarrow, strike me. My Western eyes have never seen such things before. And then there are all the trades being practiced out in the open street: the man who writes letters for those who can't, the dentist, the barber, the shoemaker. I try not to let any of the details escape me. This could have been my life.

A bowed old man comes up to offer me a drum. It is very expensive, but it is lovely. Four streets further on he is still following me because he has seen the look in my eyes and knows I have fallen for it. Faced with such insistence I start to bargain and despite my lack of talent for such things I manage to pay the amount I want to. The price includes a detailed explanation of how to play it and how to fix the leather strips it hangs from from. This way I can take it wherever I go. Most important, the old man insists, to the festivals dedicated to Ganesh.

Finally, we stop for coffee and decide to do something different: we approach the Taj Mahal hotel, probably the most luxurious in Bombay. I have to confess that since I arrived I have been thinking of coming here, but something stopped me. And now I am here. I find myself unable to move in front of the main door. For a moment I can neither go forward nor backward.

The Taj Mahal is where I used to come so often with Mother Adelina to collect leftovers from the restaurant, but obviously we didn't go in through the front door. We used to enter through the rear doors, one that led straight into the kitchens. That way you couldn't see the carpets, the vases, the furniture, the gilt fittings, the mouldings on the wall. All I saw was the enormous kitchen where they were preparing all kinds of creatures (chicken and lamb were such exotic sights to me) which I could not believe anyone was actually going to eat. A kitchen hand would help Mother Adelina load the packages into the taxi while I was usually treated to a piece of cake or some tidbit.

That is the route I should like to repeat. To go in through the kitchen entrance and go no further. Instead, I have to use the main entrance. That destitute little Indian girl has been left behind and now when I arrive at the hotel I am just another European. Without intending to, I seem to attract attention all too often, so the last thing I need to do is start asking to use the trade entrance. I would have too much explaining to do.

Once in the cafeteria, being served tea and coffee in fine porcelain, we sit and write postcards. Settled comfortably in my chair I try to imagine how to get to the kitchens and the bustle of cooks, dishwashers, pastry chefs… Perhaps there might still be someone working there, in an impeccable white uniform, who used to give me the odd piece of cake as a treat. Perhaps it might be possible to jog someone's memory. But I know it's not.

I came to India to reconstruct my past, but I realise that this doesn't mean having to retrace my footsteps in an obsessive manner. I also came here to be a volunteer. I came to learn, and I don't want to be completely absorbed in myself.

The luxury of the hotel is so disproportionate, it makes me feel ill to see such a concentration of ostentation and superficiality. The real Bombay is on the other side of the street. This is like a bubble into which the hum of real life does not penetrate.

Seeing the people who are lodged at the Taj Mahal makes me think that many of them only come here to take everything that India offers them, marvellous sights, great temples and palaces, a little exoticism, but without letting it get too close. Many of them would be so taken aback by what they saw that they are probably better off spending their holidays sealed up inside these walls, with their air conditioning, not having to tread on anything but these sumptuous carpets.

⋇⋇

We carry on with our stroll and I stop at one of the street stalls to buy a flute for charming snakes, and a violin. The flute has two pipes. At first I can't get a sound out of it, but with a little persistence I might manage to produce a note or two. Whenever I travel I find myself drawn to musical instruments and I have been slowly building up a little treasure trove. From time to time, during the music classes I give in Barcelona, I bring in one of these instruments to transport us to other countries, other music, other cultures. The flute would be a good excuse to tell the class the story of the snake charmer that my mother used to read to me when I was little.

Music has always played an important role at home. Dad is an organist and composer and Mum plays the violin. Shortly after I arrived in Barcelona they sat me on the stool in front of the piano and, without realising it, I found myself in that world quite naturally. At the same time, it was not easy because the learning process was difficult. It requires a great deal of dedication and the results only make themselves apparent in the long term. It's especially trying when your friends are going out and you must stay home, stuck in front of the piano for five or six hours a day. Persistence has its own rewards, however, and bit by bit I grew stronger until I managed to get into the Conservatory that has become my second home.

Loaded down with the drum, the flute and the violin, I must resemble a walking one-woman orchestra. Together, we walk to catch the train home and we are all in a good mood, laughing and joking, though nothing distracts my attention from the features of the men and women who cross our path. I am looking for any possible indication that one of them could be one of my parents, to whom I owe this body now wandering around Bombay and, I suppose, something more. I see them in every face. It is instinctive and I can't help myself, even though I don't actually know what I am looking for. But all of this is mere speculation. The only faces I can really see with any clarity are those of my parents who wait for me in Barcelona just as they waited twenty years ago.

Tuesday, 5th November, 1974

Dearest Asha, the days are flying by. We took you to school today for the first time. Long before you arrived here we spoke to the headmistress, Mrs Bofill, and she told us that there would be no problems, but that they would like to see you before you joined the school. And so that is what we have done. We went all the way to Sarrià and we went in together to what will soon be your new school. You seemed very put out by it. Thankfully you didn't start crying. How can I make you understand how important it is that you go to school?

We arrived during the break and when you saw all the children running into the playground, jumping and screaming, you grabbed hold of my hand fiercely and looked terrified. You must have thought it was a boarding school and you must have been afraid that we were going to leave you there. You don't have to worry, my child, I will never abandon you, only for those brief periods when it is necessary so that you can grow like any other child.

Mrs Bofill said hello to you and that seemed to calm you down a little bit. She suggested that we start as soon as possible, which means that tomorrow I am going to leave you there. For the moment it will only be for the mornings because it will take time to build up your confidence.

Wednesday, 6th November, 1974

Like all parents, we have now gone through the painful experience of leaving you at school for the first time. Well, actually, it was your father who went through it because he was the one who went with you. I stayed at home to look after your little sister. I thought about you all morning. I was worried about how you would manage, how you would be able to get along with your schoolmates as you still can't speak a word of Catalan, how you would be able to understand the teacher... Your father told me that you were crying. But at midday, when he went back to pick you up, the teacher told him you got over it very quickly and that you managed to play and draw along with the other children. When you got home you threw yourself into my arms just as you did the first day you arrived.

Before going to bed I remember that you will be seven tomorrow. I know you don't understand me, but everything is on the right track. Now you are going to school and that means I shall have a little more time to get everything done.

Thursday, 7th November, 1974
Last night, my darling girl, after saying good night, you slept uneasily and you woke up several times. The first days at school must have really disturbed you because recently you have been sleeping all through the night. Since we didn't know how to calm you down we found ourselves celebrating your birthday early in the morning. You have grown, Asha, and I hope I have the strength to be with you for many years to come, to see you grow healthy and happy. Today I thought about your parents, just as I did on the day of your sister's birthday; the parents who gave you your body, your smile, your brown skin. If they could just see you for a moment... they would be so happy to see

that you are well. At times I wonder who you look like: your mother's face, your father's eyes, your funny little nose. When you are grown up you will no doubt wonder where your features come from, your body, you will search for explanations for what you have inherited.

To your father and me, the date of your birthday will always be the 27th of October, the day you arrived in Barcelona and were born to us.

As you can imagine, it was a very agitated start to the day. After your shower you got dressed to go to school. Today, your schoolbag is filled with sweets. You were radiant and you understood that all the sweets are meant for sharing with your class.

In the afternoon we had a little party at home with the family and the neighbours in the building. On the day of Fatima's birthday you saw how the candles on the cake were meant to be blown out and so you had to blow your own out, all by yourself. Another first in your life.

You didn't want to have supper today and this time I let you off. You went straight to bed, and no sooner had you climbed in between the sheets than you went out like a light.

9

An Object of
Attention

Tomorrow it will be three weeks since I arrived in Bombay. It seems a lot longer. The days are divided among the school, life at home with the family, visits to the women's cooperative and, between one thing and another, walks through this chaotic city. The noisy racket of the crowded streets leaves me almost unable to hear myself think. All my senses overflow with the images, smells, colours, music. I pause for a moment in the middle of a street and I have a whole world around me: women busy with their bundles, a rickshaw cutting its way through the crowd, a child carrying a huge bunch of bananas on his head, a man rushing by on a bicycle, someone with a tray of tea cups.

I also see an infinite number of eyes staring at me.

In Barcelona, I look different because of the colour of my skin, my hair, my features, but because I have lived there and am now used to it, I don't notice if people are staring at me or not. As I was growing up, being different became a part of me. But now it turns out that people stare at me even here. They look at me, perplexed. We have the same skin and the same physical traits, but it is apparent that I don't really belong here. There are people who stop me on the street to ask for directions to a street or a shop and they are taken aback when they realise that I don't understand what they are saying. They must wonder: where did this one come from that she doesn't understand Marathi?

Aside from all these feelings of unease there is another question I feel obliged to resolve. Which caste do I belong to? Yes, I know the caste system has been abolished, but in practice it still applies, determining what jobs people can have, how they form personal relationships, and above all, whom they marry. Not knowing where I fit in means that I might address myself to someone I am not permitted to, or simply make a complete fool of myself. This is what happened when I spoke to some of the Indian girls working for the organisation collaborating with Setem. I asked them to tell me which caste I was. To begin with they couldn't stop laughing.

For all of my efforts to not be out of step, to get by in the most discreet possible way and without bothering anyone, I now appear to have really put my foot in it and I am not sure what I have done. When they finally manage to stop laughing, they tell me that I don't belong to any caste because I am not Indian. 'But I am,' I say, 'I was born here and lived part of my childhood here. I only want to know so that I can behave properly.' How naive!

In a more serious tone they tell me that there is nothing left about me that is Indian: 'You have dark skin, sure, and black eyes and hair, and your nose and mouth are like ours, but your demeanour has been Westernised. The only thing we have in common is our physical appearance, if that. You don't walk like an Indian, you don't look about you like an Indian, your gestures and movements are not Indian. We see you as just another European, so you don't need to worry about knowing where you belong.'

I must have been very ingenuous, because I really wasn't expecting that answer. It's one thing to notice that they look at me and treat me in a strange way, as though they don't really know if I belong here or which planet I come from, or they don't know what to make of me, but it is quite disappointing to be flat out told that I have nothing to do with this place. It is painful to feel that I have lost everything.

Before coming here, I always thought that once I set foot in this country I would be moved by a patriotic sentiment and would feel as Indian as anybody. It hasn't really been anything like that, because even if I do recognise myself in a lot of the things I see here, other things make me feel deeply indignant. Anyway, I suppose that I am the one who has to find my place and perhaps admit that I don't completely belong anywhere really, but rather a little of everywhere.

I continue on my walks through this chaotic city and the eyes of the people that I pass fix on me, again and again. Everywhere I go I feel as though I am going through a series of X-ray machines. I wear the salwar khameez and the hair that Kamal has done for me before leaving the house, all to try and adapt to my surroundings, but I can't control my demeanour. I also encounter smiles of recognition. As always, everything is mixed up together, the pain and the joy, acceptance and rejection. In any case, the curious thing is that, for good or bad, no experience leaves me indifferent. As I learn the truth about myself, the pieces that make up who I am as a person seem to fall into place.

❈

My first days in Barcelona consisted of trying to familiarise myself with my new surroundings. The first thing was to go shopping with my mother to buy warm clothes because what I had brought with me from India, despite having been bought specially, was of little use as winter drew on. As for jumpers, skirts and trousers, I was happy to try them on, but when it came to shoes, that was quite another story. I could tolerate wearing them on the street, but the moment we returned home they would go flying in different directions. What a real drama it was to get me to sit down at the table to eat. I hated all of it, because I was accustomed to an unvaried diet of rice, lentils and a few vegetables. My parents were worried because they could see that I was very thin and wanted to feed me as best they could, but there was no way of persuading me. Despite the odd episode, my adaptation actually went very quickly and smoothly. Within a week I was going to school. Since I did not know how to read or write, and certainly could not speak Catalan, at the age of seven I was put into a class of five year olds. I was queen bee because I could do all the manual tasks and drawings much better than they. The first drawing I did was hung up in the hall and all the boys and girls went to have a look. That little detail and many others like it made me feel loved and well received. As I started after term had begun, my arrival, added to the fact that I was Indian, caused quite a stir.

Without much effort I found myself speaking Catalan within three months. It is quite wonderful to think of how easy it is for children to learn a language. And I wasn't the only person who had to learn a new language. Mum is from Zamora in the central Spanish region of Castilla and she came to live in Barcelona when she was five. She had always spoken Spanish, with Dad, too. But just before I arrived, the two of them decided to make Catalan the language spoken in the house, since all teaching in the Barcelona state school system is in Catalan.

For Christmas that year I learned a Christmas carol that I sang at Mass in Vilanova de Prades, the village where my father came from. It was a frosty night and the church was quite full. When the time came, Dad gave me a signal to stand by his side in front of everyone. All wrapped up, I sang a carol about the Virgin when she was a little girl. The whole village was moved and some even had tears in their eyes to see this poor little girl who had come from the other side of the world. How well she sings it, and how she has picked up Catalan in no time at all, they seemed to say. Obviously, the words of the song had come through loud and clear!

Friday, 22nd November, 1974

Asha, my girl, each day you learn new words, and we feel lucky to be able to participate in your discoveries. We begin to understand each other and that makes everything so much easier. This is a new sensation. Well, not entirely. On the day you arrived we also felt it for a few brief moments. I don't know if I have told you this but your father was rushing about that day with a dictionary, trying to decipher what you were saying. None of it sounded English, but he persisted. Finally, in the middle of all your chatter, you said, 'put on TV' in English, and your father leapt for joy having finally understood something. That is the feeling we have now that you are beginning to say a few words in Catalan. I have read that children find it much easier to learn languages and I can confirm this now. I, on the other hand, am making very slow progress.

Today's big news is that you have started to learn to play the piano. You cried, of course, as you do whenever you start something new. I placed you on the stool and moved your fingers one by one up and down the scales. You'll soon see that its not all that difficult.

I don't want you to ever feel that you are lacking in anything compared with the other boys and girls your age.

I will do whatever I can to help you make up for lost time. You will find both of us available to give you all the help you need with your learning. Your father and I believe that the only way to achieve something that you want is with persistence, but I don't have to tell you this... since it was your stubborn determination that managed to find you a set of parents.

10

Films and Injections

I am delirious. This cold has gone on for far too long and it can't be right that I have such a bad cough and sore throat. I was going to school every day but I felt run down and was unable to put my usual energy into the activities. I didn't really pay too much attention to it at first, even though the first night I was coughing all night and from time to time I had to sit up as I felt like I was suffocating. But now with the fever it seems a lot more serious. It is never much fun being ill and even less so when you are far away from home. At one point I couldn't get up because the thermometer wouldn't drop below thirty-nine. I spent all day in bed and have been in confinement for three days now, my body weak, burning with fever and sleeping only in fits. I can't find a comfortable position to lie in, as the wooden boards of the bed stick into me through the thin mattress. My companions are keeping a close watch on me, they bring me antibiotics and cough syrup, and Kamal makes lemon drinks for me and special teas that are supposed to be miracle cures.

❧❧

Finally, as a result of the fever that comes and goes, my general indisposition, the sprints to the bathroom due to attacks of diarrhoea, and not having managed to get a good night's sleep, since the early hours of this morning I have begun to lose my sense of reality. It might be nothing more than a bad cold, as my companions tell me, but it seems that it is very resistant to the medication and I begin to suspect that I may have caught something more serious.

But that shouldn't be possible. Before I left Barcelona I made sure I had all the necessary vaccinations and I brought all the medication I needed. I try to be positive and not fall to pieces, but the fact is that it is really hard to get through these days when I'm so far away from my loved ones.

I feel very much alone. The girls spend the day out of the house, between school, yoga classes and their trips around town. Kamal boils rice for me and she occassionally changes the damp cloths that she drapes across my brow, but she has enough to see to with her own family. She is busy all day and is always on the go. The only time she stops is at night, just before she goes to bed, when she allows herself the luxury of sitting down to smoke a little tobacco paste while watching television. The one who keeps me company most is little Ibuthi. She sits on my bed and makes me little drawings to make me feel better. She is an adorable child. I look at her and I wonder if my children would turn out like her.

I have the feeling that life is running out for me and I won't be able to say goodbye to anyone. I cling to the diary I am writing. These pages could be the only account of everything I have lived through since arriving here. On the cover of my notebook I stuck two photographs that I now need to keep close to me. While I was preparing my rucksack for the journey, I went through the photo albums at home and found a wonderful picture of my parents with serene expressions lighting up their faces. I also picked out one of Fatima looking lovely. I thought they would help to keep me company and might give me some encouragement when I needed it, or when I was feeling homesick. And that is how I feel now. In these moments when I am finding it tough going, it comforts me to have them so close. I speak to all of them through the diary because I know that if I called them on the telephone and told them how I feel they would worry and that is the last thing I want them to do. Right now they are on holiday in Vilanova de Prades: hot during the day but cold enough to need a blanket at night. Dad will have gone to fetch water from the fountain and Mum will be watering the garden and Fatima practising the piano. Or perhaps they might have gone for a walk in the forest.

Now that I have managed to get myself together a little and my head has cleared slightly, I pick up the diary and write a few lines that will serve as a farewell, to show that I have been thinking about the ones I love and who have given me everything. Despite the distance, I feel them very close. I feel I am dying, and between feverish bouts of delirium, a whole film seems to pass before my eyes. It isn't the story of my life, as they say is supposed to happen to people at these times, but rather a documentary in black and white of everything I have learned on this trip and still have not digested properly. In order of appearance, there is Father Ribas, whose words managed to shake me up so much that I have been able to look at my surroundings with eyes don't judge. It is a difficult exercise and I have not always managed to achieve my objective. It's not easy to be understanding in the face of certain ways of approaching life. I have tried to live in a more spiritual way, as they do here. They can transcend life and death because one is the consequence of the other and vice versa, like the serpent eating its own tail. Taking the view that it is all part of this foreign experience does help, but adapting to it myself, the way I feel now, is more difficult. If you don't believe with firm conviction, it throws everything into doubt. It is certainly difficult to accept that there is no point in striving for anything, simply because when this life is over there will be another life to follow.

In the documentary running through my head, there are scenes when my companions from the volunteer group appear, as does everything that we have done in the work projects. The school and the cooperative: the children and the women, some of the most disadvantaged in the world. They have been an inspiration, uplifting us with their energy and the way they manage to overcome all obstacles and carry on.

And there is a special role for Mother Adelina, who shed light on so many confused memories that I had carried with me over these years. This is like a farewell. Writing in the diary puts my mind at ease because if anything happens to me, I shall leave a record of my thoughts about all the people in my life who never failed me.

Up until now, I have been patient, thinking that I would get over the coughing and shivering quickly, but I have never had a fever that has lasted so long and so have asked them to call a doctor. I have threatened to not eat anything unless they bring one soon.

Wednesday, 27th November, 1974
Today it is a month since you arrived in the house. And how much you have changed in such a short time! Now you have started eating, though from time to time you still turn your nose up at some things... Now you are beginning to have your own personal victories, like the lovely drawing you made at school which everyone admired. And you are also beginning

to make yourself understood. And all of this because you are beginning to take an interest.

Today, too, you have managed another triumph and when your father came home from work we showed it to him. You played the musical scales on the piano with both hands. When he saw you, his jaw dropped in astonishment. Sitting on the bench, you looked at us and you knew that you had made us happy. What a ray of sunshine you are! You still don't understand how much music means to us. It is something that we share and we hope that in the future you, too, might come to love it. Your father would have liked to dedicate himself to it. When I was young I studied music and the violin at the Conservatory. Encouraged by your father, I started studying again and playing the violin.

I am sure that when you start managing to produce melodies, you will realise it is worth the effort. We have noticed that you have a lot of rhythm. When your father plays, you start to dance, and you do it quite well. He spends all day admiring you both, taking photos, recording you when you speak... when he is not glued to his Super 8 camera: he catalogues all the films, and puts music on them, labels. We seem to be going through a very enriching and creative period.

Pushpa finally came to see me. When they explained my symptoms to her, she said I had probably caught malaria. But how could that have happened when I have been taking the tablets and all necessary precautions? Pushpa is the doctor at a centre where they treat people who have suffered work accidents and need immediate assistance. Last week we all went to visit the centre and she showed us around. With her I feel that I will be rescued from all the homemade remedies. Pushpa made me put on a light dress and helped me into the jeep to go to the hospital. Malaria? While we were driving I asked her all the questions I could think of. She answered without dramatising which helped to calm me down a little. She explained that some people catch malaria despite having taken the preventative medication. We parked in front of the hospital and I had to lean on her because I was so feeble that I couldn't take two steps without faltering.

The entrance to the hospital was like a movie set, and not in any metaphorical sense. Pushing open the door, we found a crane with a camera attached. The floor was covered with cables and rails for the cameras to run on. I couldn't lift my eyes from the floor because the lights blinded me. And all the actors and actresses, clad as doctors and nurses, had transformed the characteristic silence of a hospital into a total uproar. It was quite a job to find the corridor that led to a doctor who was not wearing an imitation stethoscope. There were two doors next to each other marked 'Emergency'. Pushpa opened one and it turned out to be another film set. We were almost mistaken for extras. The second attempt led us to a real waiting room, where they immediately laid me on a bed.

The doctor who examined me unleashed a torrent of questions and Pushpa had to stop him and explain that I did not speak Marathi. He was taken aback. For a moment it looked as though he wasn't sure whether or not to take us seriously, as though he thought we might have escaped from the film next door. Once everything had been explained, the doctor agreed with Pushpa and decided to test for malaria. Half an hour later the results came back from the laboratory. The test was negative, but since it is never one hundred per cent reliable they could not fully dismiss the idea. Result: I now have a ton of pills and will have to take daily injections.

Pushpa decides that I need to be taken care of properly and takes me to the residence where she works. There, I am put in with the nuns, in a room of my own. There are a few who speak Spanish and they talk to me while they prepare me a delicious soup. In the morning and at night, Pushpa comes to give me the injections. The whole centre is full of people bearing the accidents they've endured at work, and there is an atmosphere of sadness. As bad as I feel, I'm aware that I am being well taken care of and have some hope that the medicine will soon begin to take effect.

Friday, 21ˢᵗ December, 1974
Today you finished school with a folder full of your work and were happy as always. You have made a lot of progress: you can write all the letters correctly and you have also learned the numbers. We went over the exercises one by one. You are very proud of yourself.
I spoke to the headmistress about your education, and since you are doing so well, she said that next term you can move

up a class. Asha, soon you will catch up with the children of your own age. The school is happy with you and so are we. They say that you have adapted very quickly and you are putting a lot of effort into it. Now things are going to get more difficult and we can't afford to slow down. But the Christmas holidays are about to start and we can relax a bit. We will use the time to do other things.

11

Nasik

My illness has left me so exhausted that I don't have the heart to face the five hour journey to Nasik. Pushpa has just given me my injection and I feel knocked out. I get tired as soon as I stand up, and my bottom feels like a pin cushion. I have the sense that the best thing for me would be to stay here and try to recuperate. After breakfast, however, I feel a little revived and between the nuns' insistence that they will take care of me and the pressure from people in my group, I find the strength to make the trip. I have to go. How could I be so close to Nasik and not go? Nasik, the cradle where I cried the first tears of my existence, is an unavoidable step in this process of discovery; that is where the missing pieces of my puzzle rest. It might just turn out to be an excursion and nothing more, but I feel the need to reach the end. This is my last week in India and it is now or never. Who knows when I might have another opportunity to visit Nasik? The same determination which led me to climb the spiral staircase and ask for parents is helping me to fill in the blanks that have always gnawed away at me: Who were my parents? How did I end up in an orphanage? Do I have other siblings? Just as I so often give thanks for the second life I was given and ask myself why I was chosen, why I deserved the privilege and not one of the other children, I also ask the very painful question of why they abandoned me, why they didn't want to love me. Perhaps in Nasik, the silence, which has been the only answer I have known, will finally begin to respond.

Hopeful and anxious at the same time, I go to the room and put on the orange and purple salwar kameez. I run a black eye pencil over my eyes, pack a small bag and go out to the jeep.

The nuns are happy to see me so excited and explain how worried they were when they saw me arrive looking so feeble and feverish. Pushpa has prepared a package of the medicine and injections I shall need while away for the next two days. I shall have to find someone who can administer them.

Getting into the jeep, I find myself with the whole group from Barcelona. We haven't been together like this for many days and there is a lot of catching up to do on all the adventures we've been having. They are very attentive about making sure that I don't feel ill, and have saved me the seat next to the driver, Divaker – a very cheerful young man. My inner strength is all ready to go, it's just that the rest of me is not quite ready to follow. I ache all over and every movement brings moans and groans that I try not to let anyone hear.

Nasik is 184 kilometres from Bombay, but the roads are in such bad condition that the journey feels endless. A heap of destroyed cars and lorries abandoned on either side of the tarmac does not paint a very encouraging picture. We had already been told about the number of fatal accidents that have occurred on this route. I didn't pay it much attention, but now that I see it with my own eyes I am quite shocked. Divaker is singing and telling jokes but the truth is that I am suffering, because I feel very weak, because I don't know what I shall find and because everyone drives like a lunatic.

As we get further away from the city, the greens become more intense and the mountains more whimsical.

The last stretch involves traversing a steep mountain pass, one bend after another and another, until we arrive on the Nasik plain: fields and rice paddies.

Aside from my own personal research, the purpose of this trip is to visit the volunteer camp at Dindori, close to Nasik. This project consists of building reservoirs to store water from the monsoons so that it can be used during the dry season. The fact that the people have abundant water only at certain times of the year determines the way they cultivate the land and, thereby, their way of life.

The earth cannot absorb the huge quantities of water delivered by the monsoon rains and a great deal of it is lost. This runs into the rivers and from them to the sea. So, building these reservoirs will make the most of the underground water basin. The water can be pumped up from there to higher levels. This technique eliminates a lot of erosion, guarantees a supply of water until the next monsoon and helps with the cultivation of rice, which needs a lot of water during a short period.

The group working in this camp has come from Majorca and Menorca. They are headed by a Majorcan Jesuit priest named Perico Massanet, who has lived in Dindori for years and has put all of his energy into making cooperative and ecological land use possible in the area. With his team and people from the village, Massanet has managed to set up a small network of agricultural experts. They are learning new techniques and exchanging their expertise. The organisation also provides interest-free loans for people working the land who want to start up new plantations.

Perico Massanet offers us his house in Dindori for the night. Once we have sorted out who is to sleep where, I phone the convent at Nasik to tell them about my visit the next day. Everything is set up, they are expecting me tomorrow, but for now we get back into the jeep and drive from Dindori to the neighbouring village of Yambucke, where they are celebrating the Pola festival. This festival gives thanks to the cows for their help with the work in the field. They adorn them, paint their bodies with their fingers and draw patterns on their horns in very lively colours. A seemingly never-ending procession of cows and more cows is led along the esplanade.

The whole village has turned out to receive us and without doing anything I become the centre of attention. They are all looking at me, and saying things to me that I can't understand but which from their tone seem to be terms of endearment. Once more I am from here and I am not, caught in the eternal conflict between how they see me and how I feel. The fact is that I am rather proud to belong to these lands. After a first moment of awkwardness the ice breaks and everyone immediately wants to invite us to have tea with them. A man who appears to be the head of the village takes us to his house. We sit on the porch while they offer us tea, a declaration of their friendship. In this warm and inviting atmosphere we sip from steaming glasses. The setting sun provides the finishing touches to a perfect scenario. The houses, made of mud, absorb the red and copper rays of the sun. I expand my lungs as much as I can to try and draw a breath deep enough to take in all the sensations that evoke my erased past and make them a part of the present. They will now be with me forever.

In the middle of all the festival's tumult a little girl came up to me in the sqaure, took my hand, and did not leave me for a second. She didn't say anything, just stared fixedly and smiled, as if she had known me all her life. She made me feel at home but her little friends were quite jealous.

While the cows file past, the herders struggle to make them nod to us as if in greeting, while the village boys break open coconuts and hand them out to everyone. Since you cannot refuse anything that is offered to you, I accumulate an armful of coconut pieces that I can barely carry. I wander from one side of the esplanade to the other and round the temple without thinking and climb up onto a rock to get a better view. That was when I really put my foot in it! Everyone stares at me, amazed, because the rock is used for making offerings. I feel like sinking into the earth, and apologise as best I can with a lot of gesturing. In a few moments it is forgotten by all: I have the feeling they have forgiven my ignorance.

Once back at Dindori, one of the volunteers gives me my injection: Eduard, who is a vet. I freeze when I hear this, and cannot stop thinking that I am neither a cow nor a horse, and I panic that the needle might get stuck, but there is no alternative. The operation goes perfectly, without complications of any sort. After that we eat and then go to sleep. Tomorrow will be a day that I am sure I will never forget. In a matter of hours I shall arrive at the place where I was born. I can find no word to describe the kind of anxiety I feel.

The next morning, after I have spent almost the entire night awake, Toni, one of the group, offers to accompany me to Nasik. He thinks I look a little too worn out to make the journey on my own. The truth is that I feel physically revitalised and am greatly looking forward to returning to my town and visiting the nuns who took care of me until I was three. All the nervousness has taken away my appetite and I have hardly eaten any breakfast before we board the bus for Nasik. The first rays of sun reach us and the bus is now full of people and all kinds of animals.

We arrive in Nasik. I can't believe I am here. My worries lift and it feels as though all I have to do is set foot on the ground for someone familiar to come up and say hello. The emotions, the chills running up and down my spine – it's all so intense that I don't know whether to laugh or cry. Finally, I let out a peal of nervous laughter: I am laughing at myself.

Nasik is one of India's sacred cities, a place of pilgrimage. Centuries and centuries ago, the gods and the demons who had been fighting to win a jar (*kumbh*) which contained the nectar of immortality, joined forces to rescue the jar from the bottom of the sea. Once the jar was on land, Vishnu took it and fled. After twelve years of battling one another, the gods finally defeated the demons and began to drink the nectar. In the struggle, however, they spilled four drops of the precious liquid, in Allahabad, Hardwar, Nasik and Ujjain. This is why they are known as sacred cities and every three years one of the four celebrates the festival of the jar (*mela kumhba*).

I was lucky enough to have been born in a sacred city. I am sure this must have marked me in some way, like the name I was given. Asha means hope or desire. I believe that when they give you a name they are giving you a clue as to what will become of your life and certain strengths to help you achieve that. Desire and hope have always existed in my life.

The photographs and documentaries I have seen of the Ganges, the sacred river *par excellence*, now come to life in the form of the Godavari River. The Godavari traverses Nasik and along its stepped banks rise numerous temples and shrines.

In the river, women are washing clothes, and others are bathing in their saris to receive the purification of the waters. There are also funeral pyres, and just as on the Ganges, the ashes are thrown into the river. I can't stop taking photos to try and preserve a memory of each image, each moment. So many emotions are triggered by what I am seeing – the smells, the music, the water, the earth – I hope I am able to capture them in my diary, so that I can relive them in the future.

Despite the poverty, life is more dignified here than in over populated Bombay. The rhythm is more measured. How lucky that my illness did not stop me from finally coming here. Now that I am in my homeland I don't think I would ever have forgiven myself if I had missed it.

We cross the river and arrive in the market place. On one side of the square there are stalls selling fruit, vegetables, spices and clothes. On the other side are two cisterns of water from the Godavari: one for washing clothes and the other for carrying out the rituals of life and death. The men are saying their prayers. The women are washing their colourful silks and spreading them out on the ground to dry. Held down with a stone at each corner to stop them from flying away, they create a multicoloured mosaic. The children play at chasing one another around the square. All of life in this town passes through here. The sacred water cistern reflects the cycle of death, life and death again as a daily event. The people bathe in the waters which have received the ashes of the dead and so receive the spiritual life, the life of the body and the spirit.

As someone who has faith, I have found myself changing a lot of ideas that I held out of pure habit. I now see religion in a way that is broader, more spiritual and more sincere rather than dogmatic. I think of the father of the family that put us up in Bombay. Naresh never goes to the temple, he does his prayers in the kitchen at home. God is everywhere and so all you have to do is look at the sky or have a good thought in order to communicate directly with your god.

Finally, we arrive at the convent. It is like an oasis of tranquility. Luxuriant trees and abundant vegetation fill the garden with an intense green. The silence contrasts with the noise on the streets of Nasik. An arch bids me welcome. I cross under it and start up the path leading to the building, skirting past a fountain. The nuns greet me with joy, they were expecting me, and desire and reality become one: I feel at home. I was very small when I left Nasik and I have no memory of it. I don't recognise the nuns or the building, but what I sense through every pore of my skin seems familiar. The nuns talk to me in English and all of them shout my name, Asha, Asha, our little Asha, and one of them, unable to speak a word, has tears filling her eyes. It is Mother Nirmala. Between hugs and kisses, she manages to recover herself and say, 'How big you have grown... how pretty... who would have believed it!' I am surprised at how young she is, she can't be more than fifty, if that. I think she must have been very young when she took charge of me, and later when she decided to take me to Bombay and put me in the hands of Mother Adelina. She is petite, with glasses that hide her face. Almost immediately she leads me towards a little stone house just behind the convent, the place where I lived until I was three.

We sit on a bench in the garden, close to a robust tree with a swing. It is almost as if the flowers knew I was coming and decided to dress themselves in the purest white, the happiest yellow, the brightest pink and the reddest of reds. While my senses are trying to take all of this in, Mother Nirmala is staring straight at me. Before I've said one word she knows what I have come to find. With a voice that sounds as though it might break at any moment she starts to tell me the story of my past. She knows that it will be painful for me, so she dresses it up as though it were simply a story.

One stifling hot afternoon in the month of November I opened my eyes for the first time. The land in which I was born had been flooded for two months because of the torrential monsoon rains and was saturated with water. The ground longed for the first rays of the sun to break through. After the storm, the fields began to turn green. Filling the air with their intense aroma, they cried out to be sown. In those muddy stretches of water the first tender shoots of rice began to appear, a green that was fresh and new, an indisputable sign of the emergence of life. Cropping up around the square basins that were like a patchwork quilt, there emerged rounded brown hillocks, which resembled the breasts of the women who trod these humid lands, accompanied by the ring of tiny ankle bells at every step. From the break of day to the dark of night these women, small and insignificant, with bare feet and the grace of gazelles, carried the jugs full of water. Their brown bellies, the same shade as the earth, darkened by the sun, bore the shoots of new life. New babies, new fruits, new tears in an unstoppable torrent of playful laughter.

It all began and ended in a small city bathed by the cleansing waters of the sacred river of life and death. A place of pilgrimage which stands out as a magnet of supernatural attraction, whose force explains how Nasik became a cardinal point, for me as for so many other people.

At that most beautiful moment, when night and day embrace each other, in that precise instant, pleasure and pain, life and death, all come together. The testimony of life passes from one hand to the other. One is extinguished to give fruit to the other; the new arrival elbows its way in to stake its claim in a world that receives it in a hostile form.

My father, who was a farmer, was married for the second time. He had other children from his first marriage and in the context of Indian society he was quite old, around forty. When my mother died while giving birth, my father became desperate and did not have the heart to raise me. He felt old, without means, and had to take care of the children he already had; in short, my arrival posed an obstacle for him. At the end of the 1960s, Nasik was not a highly populated town, it was more like a large village where everyone knew one another and so were aware of any new births that happened. As a solution to his difficult situation, my father decided to leave me on a street corner with the hope that I would be found by someone who could take care of me. The first person who discovered me delivered me back into his arms with all manner of recriminations for his having abandoned me.

My father tried again and the result was the same, because everyone knew of my birth and which house I came from. The third time it was a nun who stumbled on that little bundle. The story of the widower who abandoned his child in desperation had passed through the entire town and over the walls of the convent. The nuns found the house and suggested that if he was not capable of taking care of me, they would do so.

From time to time a tear spills down my cheek, but there comes a point when the story is drowned out as my sobs erupt uncontrollably; they fill my chest and I can't breathe. From between the leafy trees a young nun appears carrying a tray. She offers us a jug of cold lemonade to wash away the pain.

Now, for the first time, I know where I come from. I know that I have a place of origin and I know where it is; until now my past has been a well into which you could pour bucket after bucket but it would never be filled. This pain and resentment, which for years I have put aside and ignored so as not to be impeded or conditioned by it, is all at once made real in the form of being abandoned three times. Three crosses to bear, each of them a potential threat to that most sensitive part of me, my soul. But now that I have spent three weeks immersed in this culture, so much a part of me and yet so foreign, I understand the attitude of a devastated man who, in unfavourable circumstances, had to bear the loss of his wife and my arrival, which, rather than being a joy to him, represented a heavy burden.

Clearly, it is difficult to comprehend, but Mother Nirmala gives me the tools to see it with Indian eyes, in its own context. These facts have marked my existence, otherwise I would not be here trying to decipher the tortuous paths which led me to a second life. Between all the crying and the effort required to absorb so much information, so many conflicting sentiments, there is also room for more cheerful anecdotes. Mother Nirmala tells me about Johnny, the little boy I used to play with. She points to the swing, which is only a few years old, and says that if that swing had been there when Johnny and I used to run about this garden, we would have managed to break it. We were little rascals and didn't think twice about anything, just carried on with one prank after another until we could get the nuns to give us a treat for our amusing antics.

When I was three years old, the nuns decided to send me to Regina Pacis in Bombay. I would be able to go to school there. They would teach me and prepare me for the moment when I was grown up and ready to spread my wings and fly on my own. None of them ever imagined in their wildest dreams that their little girl, that busy little bee, would fly so high and so far away.

As I look out at the garden, sitting there on the bench next to Mother Nirmala, it feels almost as if time has stopped. I see the trees, the new swing which wasn't there twenty years ago, the flowers… and I imagine chasing barefoot after Johnny, in that funny way little creatures run. This is the frame of the first chapter of my life, it is real. But I still need the last pieces of the puzzle, those which will give it its final shape and ensure that it is never incomplete again. They are in the Church of Saint Anne where I was baptised. Mother Nirmala goes with me, as does Toni, who has been taking photos of us since we got here. We walk there as it is only a few metres from the convent, and on the way, she explains that she made the dress for my baptism, covered in ribbons and bows with no detail spared. My godfather was the father of one of the nuns, and the sister of another acted as godmother. After the ceremony there was cake for everyone.

Father Prakaast receives us warmly and pulls the registry book from a cupboard. While he prepares a copy of the baptism certificate I have asked him for, I sit beside him and let my eyes run over the lines written on my page:

Date of baptism: 7th May, 1969. Date of birth: 7th November, 1967. Name: Asha Maria. They kept the name I had been given at birth and added Maria to make it Christian. Surname: Ghoderao. Father's name: Radhu Kashinath. When I reach the sixth line my eyes fill with tears as I read the letters one by one that make up the name of the woman who gave her life in giving birth to me: Shevbai. I ask the priest to pronounce, in his language, the names of the people who were my parents. I have never seen them, nor will I ever see a single picture of them, but just hearing the music of their names helps me to construct an image. Father's profession: Farmer. Nationality: Indian. Then come the names of the godparents, the chaplain and the place where I was baptised: the Church of Saint Anne in Nasik.

The mists that shrouded my origins have lifted. I am walking through the town where I was born. I know how I ended up at the convent and how I got from there to

Bombay to fly on to Barcelona. All the gaps have been filled with words and specific images that describe my reality.

Nobody ever spoke to me about my father. A few years after I arrived in Barcelona, Mother Adelina wrote to tell us of his death. The death of my father was the only news I ever had of him, and despite never having known him, remembering nothing, feeling only rancour towards him, I was still very sad. Of my mother I knew even less. I tried to find her among the women I saw on the streets of Bombay. I would fix on a sari of bright silk, a pair of penetrating eyes, an elegant walk, and I wanted to find something familiar. If only I could see her, just for a second.

Somewhere I have some siblings. I don't know how many, or if they are boys or girls, or what kind of life they have, if they have children, where they live, how they live. They are the children of my father's first marriage. Mother Nirmala, however, advises me not to look for them. They know nothing of me, they were told nothing and they have their own lives. She thinks that our encounter might disturb them and she might be right. So, I should not worry about it any more and ought to put an end to my research into the past.

12

Back From India

It has taken me seven years to try to put the notes of my travel diary into some kind of order, and to re-read them calmly. After I returned from India I needed a couple of months to get my emotions sorted out and carry on with my life. It was not easy. In repeating the magical route I had made twenty years ago, from Bombay to Barcelona, I was taking the first step towards digesting everything I had discovered. Every bit of pain, every spark of joy which emerged in India is now trying to settle inside me. I absorbed everything like a sponge, open to it all. And really, none of my experiences were in vain. I have grown as a person.

Of course, changes don't happen just like that. The act of filling the gaps, of finding answers, has allowed me to find myself, to form a more solid identity. Now I know that I also belong to the wonderful land of India, and it is wonderful not because everyone says so, but rather because in many ways I felt just like another Indian; I was happy to be a part of it. Now that everything is in order, I can look back at the past and feel moved. I can talk about my story, and I can look to the future and make decisions which may or may not be right, but I am no longer floating about in uncertainty. One of those decisions was to write these pages. I needed to explain myself.

Before going back to India, I watched every television documentary about the country. At first, with my parents and Fatima, and later in my own place. If necessary, I would record them to avoid missing any, but I didn't feel prepared to go into it any deeper, to get to know people who could tell me about my country in their own words. I always ended up asking what would have become of me had I stayed there. I felt privileged and guilty, and that prevented me from finding the courage to learn any more. Now I feel proud to be an Indian-Catalan, and I no longer lower my gaze when I meet people from my country. On the contrary, there is mutual recognition. Moreover, the mixture allows me to carry on as I am. I grew up here, but a lot of what I am comes from over there, and I don't simply mean the physical aspects. During my stay in India I recognised an infinite number of details in myself, such as the way I had always liked walking around barefoot, the smell of incense, striking colours, the harmony of flowers and candles.

Coming back to Barcelona also opened my eyes to another reality. There was a whole movement of people adopting children from other countries. I felt obliged to tell my story. I couldn't just keep it to myself because I had taken as much as I could from it. With my experience I could show people that even though things looked complicated they could turn out well in the end. So I offered to do a few talks for those just starting out on the road to adoption. The adoptive parents-to-be arrived at my talks in low spirits. They were bewildered by the long application process. It all looked like an impossible mountain to climb, and they were having doubts. I tried to allay their fears, explaining how natural parents ultimately also go through the same process: they make their decision with all the good will in the world and then they have nine months to go through all the worries, to be scared, to stop being scared, to ask themselves if they know what they're doing. But no child arrives with a set of instructions, and neither do the adopted ones. Many of the things they were concerned about had no clear answer, almost nothing is cut and dry, but there is one thing which I am adamant about: the changing of children's names. There is always the excuse that perhaps they will be given a child with a difficult name to pronounce, or that sounds strange in the language of their newly adopted country. In my view, you can't change anyone's name. When you are born, you are given a name and there is always a reason. That name is a part of you, it goes everywhere with you. If they had changed my name it would have been an attempt to erase seven years of my life. This child is going to face enough challenges, a new country, language, customs; how can he or she deal with another change? The hope concealed in my name has been my guide, the impulse that has seen me through since I was very small.

The general desire is to adopt babies. By telling my story, I help them see that adopting children who are a little older is not an insurmountable problem. Those children are very aware of their situation and they deserve an opportunity. There is also a lot of concern about language and there are parents who immediately think of sending the children to an international school. My feeling is that if children are to feel they belong, they must be integrated into their environment right from the start. They will learn other languages when the time comes.

Their previous life has to be put to one side without rejecting it. Their natural parents have to be present in some way, but they should never be blamed for abandoning them. No secrets, and no rancour. It can be difficult to strike the right balance between explaining where a child comes from and their integration into a new family, with all that this entails. Normally, the child will mark the pace, in the way they express interest or curiosity. When I was small I used to feel terrible panic when I saw people from India, thinking they would take me away with them. Other children might not be so concerned, every person is different. What you cannot do is force them to either forget or to remember more than they do.

Returning to one's place of origin is also something that worries parents. They want to know when it should be done and how. Again, it should not be forced. Above all, the children have to feel secure that their new parents will not let them down. I didn't feel capable of doing this until I was twenty seven years old. Others are ready for it much earlier, it all depends. My sister Fatima, for example, still doesn't even want to talk about going back to India. It's true that the pain of thinking about how you were abandoned is intense and not easily allayed.

Sometimes I meet adoptive parents-to-be who ask me about racism, about adolescence, about all that can happen and everything that can affect you. I tell them personal anecdotes, but ultimately the message has to be that they should put aside their worries, because in the end everything will turn out well in this adventure of love.

I would like this book to be my little contribution to those people who find themselves going through what my parents and I went through. I feel the need to explain myself and at the same time to put my experience at the disposal of those to whom it could be useful. After reading it, future parents might be able to put some of their fears in proportion. For those who have already formed a family, perhaps they might see in this a reflection of some of their own experiences; possibly their stories have taken a completely different course, but equally enriching. This is why I have included some fragments from my mother's diary as a counterbalance to everything that I experienced. The story seen from the other side. Two separate points of departure, at times opposing, but which finally merge together.

For now, however, I can only hope that it will not be another twenty years before I visit India again.

Barcelona, August 1995 – September 2002

Part Two:

The Other
Face Of
The Moon

1

Returning to my Origins

I am returning to India again, much sooner than I had expected. It will be my second journey back to the country where I was born. Almost thirty years of life in Barcelona have passed since the first time I arrived there in 1974 from Bombay (when it was still Bombay; now it is Mumbai).

Before I went back to India the first time in 1995, the questions I wanted to answer were my own. My concerns were silent and difficult to share, very solitary. It was a few years later that I began to realise that I was not alone and that my questions were neither unique nor restricted to me. As I got to know other adopted people, younger than me, I discovered that they were all asking the same questions I had once asked myself.

When we were small, Fatima and I were the only touch of colour in our family circle, in school, in our neighbourhood. Now, in the new millennium, mothers and fathers going into this kind of adoption are very well prepared, they have strong social support and information. They can contrast and discuss their experiences with a lot of other families. They can find books on the subject and consult loads of Web sites on the internet. They can attend discussion groups with adoptive parents from all over the world.

The most important thing, however, is that adopted boys and girls are beginning not to feel all that different, all that special. Particularly when, from time to time, they meet other children who come from the same country of origin. They grow up knowing that there are others who are living the same adventure as them, and in some way I think that the life they have seems easier. To be able to share the experience of being different, as they do now, must be much more pleasant.

There is no comparison between the way adopted boys and girls are brought up today and how they were a few decades ago, when there wasn't a single children's book that dealt with the differences, when the only thing that counted was the intuition of the parents, who were veritable pioneers. There are always exceptions, but I believe I can say that the new generations of adopted boys and girls live right from the start with a knowledge of their own stories, short or long. Many of them are prepared to go back to seek their origins, even if they finally decide not to repeat the experience, either out of fear of being confronted with their past, or for some other personal reason.

So much has changed since my first journey back to India. I get chills just thinking about it. It was quite unthinkable to me that the publication of *Daughter of the Ganges* would bring me into the lives of so many people. Their fascinating stories, without their realising it, have helped me to better understand who I am and what it means to be an adopted child.

Now I am going to go back to Mumbai and to Nasik, the town where I was born, in order to transform the story I wrote into images, to convert it into a documentary for television. And it is in this moment that I recall all the questions I had before stepping aboard the plane to make my first journey. I remember the worries I had and how nervous I was about returning to the country where I was born: the anxiety of meeting once more the nuns who had taken care of me in the early years of my infancy; the doubts I had about whether I would be able to speak Marathi. More than anything, I remember the worries

I had about finding out what had happened at the very beginning of my story, why I had been abandoned. This and many other questions were what I carried with me in my suitcase on that first trip. This time I don't have so much baggage with me (or so I think).

When I went back to my country of origin a second time, I knew before I set out that I would probably pick up on things I hadn't seen the first time, that a lot of small details must have passed me by. The reasons for this trip are different. Now I am going back to film a documentary about my book, but I also have a secret purpose: to track down someone from my biological family.

A few days ago I received an e-mail from Nirmala in Nasik. I had to read it several times before I began to take it in. Nirmala is one of the nuns who took care of me when I was small and her e-mail, which was a bit confused and written in a strange kind of Spanish, seemed to suggest that she knew something about my story that she had never told me. So, once again I am going to board a plane for India with another knot in my stomach, with serious doubts about whether I shall be capable of facing a new set of emotions.

My first journey back to India was undertaken with the good company and understanding support of a group of NGO volunteers. This time I am lucky enough to be travelling in good company again. Coming with me are Jordi Llompart, who will direct the documentary; Mikele López and Grau Serra, the two wonderful cameramen; and Anna Soler-Pont, my literary agent, who is one of the people responsible for so many of the things that have happened to me since the publication of *Daughter of the Ganges*.

This is the beginning of a double adventure: the challenge of making a documentary and the will to follow through with the research into my origins. It is now that I realise that one single journey was not enough.

2

Everything in its Proper Place

The first time I went back I also began in Mumbai, partly to get used to the reality of India, but also because that was where the volunteer work I had come to do was being organised. Then, I was lodged with the Patil family. This time I am staying in a hotel in Colaba, which is called downtown although it is far from everything, the most remote point on any map of the city. The hotel is by the sea, very close to the Gate of India, one of the monuments that evokes the era of British colonisation, and the luxurious Taj Mahal Hotel.

On the day after arriving in the city, we pass in front of the Gate of India early in the morning on our way to Regina Pacis to begin filming the documentary. Things are different now because Mother Adelina died in the year 2000. I didn't find out until just before I set out on this trip and it was quite a blow. Mother Adelina will always be one of the most important people in my life. It was she who did her utmost to make the dream I had when I was five years old finally came true: to have a mother and a father. She was one of the nuns at Regina Pacis, the convent where I lived from the age of three to six, and it was from there that I went to meet the people who became my parents.

The whole team (Jordi, Mikele, Grau, Anna and me) goes in two taxis loaded with all the equipment for filming: metal boxes filled with lights and tripods are loaded onto the roof racks and practically sink the cars, old as they are, and the overloaded boots have to be tied up with string. We pass in front of the two stone lions which still stand guard at the entrance to the main station in Mumbai: Victoria Terminal. The area in front of the building, inspired by the English colonial style, or perhaps an actual copy of a real building in London, is crowded with street vendors. The chaotic traffic brings us to a halt which allows me to take a closer look at all that is going on in the streets in front of the station. A boy approaches the window of my taxi and puts his hands to his mouth to indicate that he wants something to eat. *Chapati* is the only word I understand of what he says. I remain fixed, staring at him with all the sadness in the world, immobile. I sit there, stuck to the seat of the car, and feel powerless. A sea of black and yellow taxis, similar to those in Barcelona, moves slowly forward, hooting their horns. A sea of noise, unbearable. On one side a motorcycle comes by with a whole family on board. The father is driving with a boy of about seven in front of him, holding tightly to the handlebars; the mother, dressed in a sari, is sitting side-saddle on the back with a young child in her lap; and between father and mother, a little girl no more than four years old. Of course, not one of them is wearing a helmet. On the other side a bicycle appears, loaded down with live chickens. Along the pavement are stalls selling everything, lined up one after the other: piles of shoes of every kind, cut watermelons covered with flies, sugar cane or sugar cane juice, schoolbags, white cotton shirts, coconuts, pirate CDs... There are also lots of tobacco stalls set up on every corner with baskets of eggs hanging from the roof, which you often see. They are building everywhere and lots of people live between the heaps of debris piled on the construction sites, where they can stay until another building starts and forces them off. The cars dodge around the fires they use for cooking and for keeping warm at night.

Having crossed half the city, drinking in images of all kinds, I glimpse the imposing wrought iron gate. To the right is the sign that has always been there, with the name which now seems like a frontier I had to cross to get from one place to another, from one country to another, from being an orphan to having a family. Regina Pacis. The two taxis stop and we start to unload the equipment. The asphalt on the road has deteriorated and there are big puddles everywhere. We will spend the day filming here. My heart is beating. Anna goes up to say hello to Margaret Fernandes, the nun who is in charge of the convent, the girls' orphanage, the home for destitute girls, and the school for poor girls. This order of nuns was founded by Vicenta María López Vicuña in Madrid in 1876. The first four Spanish nuns arrived in India in 1951.

When I can, I get away by myself and go straight to the big hall where I slept as a child. The same fans are still on the ceiling. I remember staring at them while they turned, which would help me to sleep.

Everything is the same, except that Mother Adelina is no longer here. The crows in the branches of the trees cry out the same way they did when I was little. Seeing them, I can't help thinking of the time when one of them attacked me while I was living here. There are a lot of flowers of every colour. It is monsoon season and between the abundance of rain and the constant heat, the garden is in full bloom.

I climb the steps to the main entrance and ask for Margaret. I ask in an English that I am hoping to improve soon. In the entrance hall, with all the dark wooden furniture and the ceiling fans, I am immediately taken back to my childhood, to all the times I had crossed that space running barefoot. It hasn't changed at all. It smells the same. It smells clean.

My meeting with Margaret begins to dislodge a few of the details of my story. Margaret is from Goa, the old Portuguese colony in India, and apart from Portuguese and English she speaks Spanish very well. She was at Regina Pacis when I used to live here. A few months ago I sent her a copy of my book in Spanish and she read it straight away. She has been hoping to discuss it because she claims it is full of mistakes. I feel a mixture of shame and anger. Mistakes? Yes, and as far as she is concerned, some of them are quite serious.

I came prepared to experience some powerful emotions, but I wasn't prepared to hear that there were things in my book that were not correct. The first thing Margaret tells me is that Regina Pacis never had rich girls and poor girls as I had thought. Margaret tells me that all the interned girls – the ones who were not orphans, who I remembered having received visits from their parents – were girls from families with no resources and that some of them received visits from a parent only once a year. She also strongly insists that there were no differences between what the orphan girls ate and what the interned girls ate. Also, when I was small, the food that I used to go and collect from the kitchens of the hotels along with Mother Adelina was to supplement everybody's food. I listen to what she has to say so as not to contradict her, but my own memory is very clear. Isn't the matter of whether you sleep in a bed or sleep on the floor on top of a towel enough indication of difference?

But if that were the only thing, I would not have minded. She goes on to tell me that my father did not abandon me but handed me to the nuns to ensure that I would have a better future than the one he could offer. To abandon someone is too strong a concept and Indians would never do that to their children. Rather, they hand them to someone who can look after them when they are not capable of doing so themselves. I try to think about the difference between abandoning children and handing them over, and I find it difficult. Margaret says that my father, Radhu Ghoderao, loved me a lot, so much so that he came to Mumbai to see me before I was adopted by my parents in Barcelona, but I did not recognise him. 'Who is this man?' Mother Adelina asked me. 'The postman!' I apparently answered. The scene took place at one of the tables in the room we are sitting in now.

But why didn't they tell me all this before? I feel like laughing and crying at the same time.

Margaret was not here the first time I came back to India. Then, I spoke only to Mother Adelina, who knew about my origins but refused to give me the information I asked her for. Each time, she told me that it was better not to stir up the past, that I had to look forward, that the past could only do me harm and that I had the best possible life I could ever have wished for. It was no use insisting that I wanted to know more about my story. Mother Adelina believed it was better for me not to know any more of my story and I accepted that.

Now, some years later, I find it difficult to understand how Mother Adelina managed to conceal such an incredible anecdote. I can't deny the anger that I feel. A father – my father – who travelled all the way to the city to see his daughter for the last time before she set off for a distant country to be adopted by a family, is an image from my story that is completely unknown to me and has a huge impact. I can't imagine how that man must have felt, poor, tired, a widower, travelling all the way to the big city to say farewell to me and to see me one last time.

Why should a child who has lived in a convent or an orphanage have to lose their story? Does their past have to be wiped out completely? It is difficult for me to accept that some people think that everything should be erased.

❦

Margaret is prepared to help me and goes on to tell me everything she knows. Radhu, my father, wore a white turban, a *pheta*, like many men who work on the land. And the postman who appeared from time to time at Regina Pacis also wore one and that was probably why I confused them. I imagine him travelling from Nasik to Mumbai, walking into this room on a morning just like today, with the fans turning and the same smell of old wood, knowing that he would see his daughter for the last time, supposing that she would probably not recognise him. My eyes are brimming with tears.

In her cold, forceful manner, Margaret tells me that when my father gave me to the nuns in Nasik, I had a sister a little older than me, a girl who in those days was about five, or perhaps a little younger. Margaret wasn't there but thinks that she recalls Nirmala and Mother Adelina explaining how that little girl had been present at the time of the handover and that they had seen her a couple of times afterwards. I feel a chill go through me. A girl who accompanies her father to leave her little sister in a strange place because they don't have the resources to take care of her themselves is an even sadder and more striking image.

What was that girl thinking? And where is she now? If she is still alive, would she remember me? Each new phrase of Margaret's diminishes me, makes me feel smaller and more insignificant.

The surprises do not end here. Now it turns out that we do not come from Nasik, the sacred city on the banks of the river Godavari, a place of pilgrimage which has become, to me too, an important point of reference, but rather from another, smaller village. Margaret doesn't even know its name. It is all too much for me. Too many things to take in. The ceiling fans turn, but the heat, which has never bothered me before, now seems to take effect. For a few moments I think I might faint and fall flat on the floor.

What about Nirmala? She was the one who told me all about my story in Nasik. Why didn't she tell me everything? Why did she tell me that I had been born in Nasik? And where did she get the idea that my father, Radhu, had tried to abandon me in the street, hoping that someone would pick me up, before bringing me to the convent on his third attempt? Where did that story come from? Whom was I to believe?

Now I want to know everything exactly as it was. I recover from the shock with a glass of cold water. I sense that there are a lot of new things to discover and for the first time someone is trying to tell me the truth. I want to know exactly what happened from the time I was born until the moment my father entrusted me to the nuns. I want to know exactly where I was born and what happened to that little girl who was my sister. I want to know why they separated us. I want to know if I have other siblings and what their lives have been like. I want to find it out now while I am here, but if it can't be done then I will come back to India as many times as it takes. I realise that it is now more important than ever to try to reconstruct my past and that of my biological family. I don't know why, but I need to do it.

I ask Margaret to help me find out all this information. I don't hesitate for a second. In a few days we will be in Nasik and there I shall meet Nirmala. This time I shall tell her that I want absolutely all the details of my story. Margaret apologises, saying that I am not the only child who has been adopted from the orphanage and that a lot of years have gone by and it is not easy to retain the details of every story perfectly. Nobody bothered to write down my story nor that of any of the other girls, nobody took the time to note all the dates, names and facts with precision. The passing of time erases everything if nothing has been registered in any way.

I am afraid. I am afraid that I am not going to like what I find. For several years now I have believed that I had made sense of my story, everything was in its proper place, and I felt at ease with the past. I told my story to a lot of people and even wrote it down. Now I feel as though I am on the edge of a precipice, about to jump out into the void.

I think about my parents, Josep and Electa, and the care with which they have always guarded all the documents of my adoption. And of the diary which my mother kept precisely so that I might find the answers to all the questions I might have. At least everything that I experienced from the age of almost seven, when I arrived in Barcelona, was written down by my mother and filmed and photographed by my father, and now I am more grateful to them than ever.

Margaret accompanies me on my visit around the Regina Pacis grounds, I feel like seeing it all one more time. They are about to pull down one of the buildings, the oldest and nicest of all of them, built in a colonial style, with carved wooden windows and railings and lovely columns. It is falling to pieces, everything is propped up and they don't have the resources to restore it. It's a real shame. The demolition work will start in a few days' time and several nuns are busy carrying out boxes full of papers and books as they empty the rooms.

We have to film the scene on the spiral staircase. I climb the rickety wooden stairs once more, barefoot, just as I did when I was small. Halfway up I have to make an effort not to start crying. Each step still creaks, just as I remember. For me, this staircase will always be the symbol of the beginning of my second life. All of us who have been adopted have a scene like this saved in our memory that reminds us of the very beginning of everything. At the top of the staircase I sit down on a step in front of the chapel, exactly as I did the first time I waited for Mother Adelina to finish her prayers so that I could ask her to find some parents for me.

✦

I visit two rooms where they are having classes. The girls sit barefoot on the floor, with their exercise books on their knees. Their shoes are lined up in a row outside. The youngest girls sing some songs for me. The majority of them are orphans; some were brought there by their parents, just as I was, girls with parents who live in some corner of India but are incapable of feeding them properly, and even less capable of giving them an education. Girls whose families live in the streets. I can't help feeling moved by this. I am one of them, I was there once. Perhaps I too sang a song for a visitor one day, while I was sitting there in class barefoot – on one of the few days when I was not playing truant – and I would have observed the guest with the same dark and profound gaze with which these girls

143

are now watching me. There is something familiar about it, the knowingness of someone who has already seen a lot. It is not the innocent, infantile gaze of a child, but one which freezes your blood and makes you think.

I play a piece on the old Regina Pacis piano for the nuns. Tremulous, emotional, but I manage to get through it. It is my way of thanking them for their time. The piano is one of the symbols of my life in Barcelona, the legacy of my adoptive parents which has turned me into a music teacher for the last thirteen years.

We wrap up the day's filming with tea and biscuits together in the small hall where the wooden spiral staircase begins. And the parting is not painful at all. I know that I shall be back again, and I have really begun to feel that I belong to this place too.

3

Seeing Mumbai With New Eyes

I wander from one side of Mumbai to the other, observing everything in a different fashion to the first time I came back. I am no longer searching for something of myself among the glances of the people here, nor do I examine the women looking for one who might resemble my mother. I feel much calmer, and what I see, even though it is still hard to witness the misery, the injustice, the abysmal differences between people, I absorb much more serenely. The only note of unease I feel is when I think of everything that Margaret told me, and all that I have to reconstruct in the story of my life. Instead of my mother, I am now looking for my sister in the women I see in the streets. Do we look alike? How has her life been? Might she too have ended up being adopted by a family far from India? Or a family here in Mumbai? I would really like to meet her again, and I look for her everywhere.

⚛

We have filmed some sequences in the neighbourhood of Bandra and in other parts of the city. It is late Sunday afternoon and we are returning, tired after a long day of shooting. The immense piles of rubbish covered with crows, dogs and the occasional scurrying rat, can be seen on the same stretch of street, only a few metres away from children's clothes shops, shoemakers, dental clinics, top class film producers' offices and vegetarian restaurants where we can eat really well. I walk along the streets of the city dressed in Indian clothing, with lively colours and big earrings. I know that even though I might appear very Indian, people can tell from some way off that I am not from here. This time, however, I am taking it much more lightly and have not been as affected by this. My gestures, the way I walk, and above all, the way I act, are completely Western. I know this now and do not try to pretend otherwise. It is the way we look at things, ultimately, which differentiates us from people living on the other side of the world. For the first time I maintain the pleasing sensation of walking through the streets of Mumbai without feeling any anxiety. I am no longer afraid of this city.

⚶

Andheri is a popular quarter of Mumbai, forty kilometres from Colaba. The two hour ride by taxi from the hotel provides a constant spectacle of life in its rawest form; movement, action, people on the move, at work. Most of the roads were built many years ago and the asphalt has some very big holes in it, while others are covered with earth or filled with pools of rainwater. Motorcycles are the most predominant vehicles, along with bicycles and auto-rickshaws, which are forbidden in other neighbourhoods closer to the centre. There are rickshaws piled high with all manner of things, cardboard boxes that protrude from all sides... There are a few handcarts pulled by men on foot. It is very hot, the pollution is very dense, and the horns are beeping desperately, constantly. A huge poster announces the latest arrival from Hollywood, *Matrix Reloaded*, which sits alongside a large, hand-painted advertisement for Indian soap. I notice it because there are a dozen men adding the finishing touches, working with their pots of paint and brushes atop one of those scaffolds that seem to break every safety regulation in the book – they're made of bamboo canes and wooden boards tied together with rope.

In Andheri I looked up the Patil family, who put me up during my first stay here in 1995. We filmed several scenes in their home, remembering and reconstructing the intimate and intense moments we shared there. The mother and father, Naresh and Kamal, haven't changed a bit. Naresh is still driving a taxi and working all the hours he can to give his three daughters the best possible life. Kamal, elegant as always in her sari, continues to busy herself with the logistics of the household, ensuring that everything runs smoothly. Every meal requires many hours of preparation, as well as the time it takes to go by foot to buy the ingredients or, if Naresh takes a few hours off, to take the taxi a little further away. Her vegetables with rice and her lentil soup – the famous *dhal* – are unbeatable.

Nanda, the eldest girl, is now twenty-five and works as a receptionist in a hotel by the sea, though she is qualified in both psychology and sociology from the University of Mumbai and speaks very good English. She is looking for a better job but hasn't found one yet. She dresses in a Western manner. She doesn't like saris because they get in the way. She wears the *salwar kameez* only when she is in the house, and occasionally in the street. She is in no hurry to find a partner and start a family, even though she knows this is her parents' dream. She tells me that she has discussed the subject countless times with her parents and they have decided to let her choose whom she wants. She says that times have changed and nowadays you can't force children to marry someone the parents want, even though it remains a very common practice. Nadina is now twenty and graduated from university a few months ago. Every week she buys a paper called *Employment News* to look for a job, but she hasn't found anything yet. She would like to work in an office. The one who has changed the most is Ibuthi: the little girl I knew has turned into a teenager. She still walks to school every day and still dreams of being a dancer.

It is impressive to see how all five of them manage to live in harmony in such a small space, with little electric light, two sofas in the room which serves as the parents' bedroom at night and a living/dining room during the day, one room for the three girls, the kitchen – where there is a little temple dedicated to Ganesh and Sai Baba – and a tiny bathroom without much to offer.

The three girls and I eat together on the floor of the main room. The television is on because the most important series is airing. It has been running for more than six years without interruption. We eat with our hands. My problems with eating rice with my hands have gone. When I first arrived in Barcelona I didn't know how to use a knife and fork and my mother found it fascinating to see how skilful I was at eating with my fingers.

On this occasion, even more than when I was living here as an extra member of the family, I feel that my life could also have been like this. A simple Indian family with its daily struggles that somehow seems to thrive.

Above all, accepting that times change and that customs and needs have also changed.

Without warning, a downpour descends on us, as if someone has opened the gates of a hidden dam. A curtain of water falls in a fury on the improvised shelters built against the walls of the Jeja hospital in blue, black and yellow plastic. Many families live there, having paid to occupy a place in the city, even if it is covered by nothing more than a sheet of plastic. The water has caught us in the middle of filming and we worry about the cameras. Mikele and Grau react quickly, putting up umbrellas and waterproofs in the middle of the street. Their sense of humour proves indispensable in moments like this. The small kids run around amusing themselves while the women carry on walking up the street, unperturbed and elegant beneath their colourful umbrellas. The seven o'clock bells of the evening *puja* can be heard from the little temple in the hospital grounds. The red double-decker buses are filled to capacity, their windows completely misted up. It is a Muslim quarter and the goats wander about freely, nibbling on everything they can find in the huge piles of rubbish, even the occasional table of a street stall, or the handle of a cart. On the balconies of the small Parijath Hotel on the other side of the street some people can be seen watching the rain. Those riding bicycles are completely soaked, pedalling with their shirts stuck to their bodies.

I call Nirmala and Margaret to ask if they have anything more to tell me. Nirmala is happy to hear from me and from the tone of my voice seems to understand that this time I need to know all the details of my life. Margaret has passed the news on. Nirmala has also read my book and found inaccuracies in it. She remembers having told me my story just as it was and doesn't understand where I found the ideas for what I wrote. I tell her that it makes no sense for me to invent things. The confusion is mutual, but there is a lot of affection and we both want to see each other again.

I realise that the last time I went to see her I took her by surprise. There was no time for her to prepare, to gather all the information. I suppose that I myself wouldn't have been able to remember the stories of so many girls with any accuracy. She has asked someone to help her to enquire about my sister or anyone from my biological family as thoroughly as possible. The knots in my stomach start acting up again. The image of that little girl saying goodbye before leaving me with complete strangers is with me all the time.

❀

The school where I worked as a volunteer in the neighbourhood of Andheri in 1995 is different than it was. The name remains the same, Jeevan Nirwaha Nirketan, which in Marathi means 'a school for life'. They have put up a new building to teach many more underprivileged boys and girls; kids who work all hours of the day have a chance to spend a few hours studying here. Many of the children and adolescents live in the orphanage of Saint Catherine's, which is in the same grounds as the school and has been there for many years. When we enter through the main gate with the two taxis loaded down as always with all the film equipment, the guard makes us sign in and I notice the name of one of the visitors in the book who had signed in earlier that morning. As a reason for their visit they wrote only one word: 'adoption'. From the name I imagine they are English, or perhaps American.

While Mikele and Grau are busy filming Jordi interviewing some boys and girls picked from the classrooms in the school, Anna and I talk to some of the others, adolescent girls mostly. Sitting on the ground in the yard, we listen to their stories and answer the questions they have about us. Most of them are orphan girls, some of whome never knew their parents. Many have always lived there and were found by the nuns at the gates of the Saint Catherine convent or the Bal-Bhavan orphanage nearby; others were orphaned only recently and are interned in the orphanage because their families cannot look after them any longer... It is surprising how they are able to tell their stories with such ease, and how curious they are to hear mine.

Deepa is one of the older ones. She is fifteen and was found at the gates of the orphanage, where she has lived ever since. She tells me that she had a friend who was taken far away from India by European parents and that she never heard anything from her after that. And that over the years she had seen how people had come for other children and she could never understand why no one ever came to fetch her. What was the reason why some children were chosen to go to live with a family while others were not? She remembers all the girls she spent her childhood with and wonders what has happened to them. She also knows that some of them were adopted by families in Mumbai.

4

Usha and the Sacred City

The first time I came back to India I was incapable of seeing some of the things I am seeing now. We have filmed scenes in the poorest parts of Mumbai. We have visited orphanages and talked to girls with all kinds of stories to tell, some of them very sad. Seeing them that first time made it much harder for me to bear my good fortune of having been adopted than it is now. But the key question continues to press itself: why me?

Seeing the child prostitutes on the streets broke my heart, but now I can see their situation more objectively. Up until now I always felt too involved. I identified with it so much that I couldn't bear it. This time I have seen not only the poorest, most raw aspects but also the people who are struggling. I have been able to see close up how the new generations of women have many more possibilities, like the three Patil daughters. The girls in the Andheri school appear nothing like those I saw on my first visit. The only thing I recognised that time was their will to survive. Now, I see they want to live with dignity, they have more ambition and wish to be trained for stimulating professions. The last time, I didn't speak to the girls, particularly the older ones at the orphanage. What I saw and felt then were as much as I could take.

But now I had more information and I felt more sure of my story, I wanted more. Once I had overcome the fear of what I might find, I was capable of going one step further and confronting anything. And then I had to be very insistent to attain the truth about my adoption. Those people who had information about the past might remember different versions of the facts, as there is never one single version.

❧

On the road to Nasik we film a few scenes for the documentary. The road begins in Mumbai and ends in Agra, the city of the Taj Mahal. Anna is inside the jeep parked on the side of the road, a white Toyota laden down with film equipment and our luggage. She is busy making one phone call after another on her mobile telephone, trying to set up filming for the coming days. Suddenly, during a break, she comes over to speak to me. Something is happening. I can see it in her face which looks as though she is either about to smile or burst into tears. We both sit down inside the white Ambassador, a car that has an elegant, antique look about it, which the Indians usually hire as taxis for long distance journeys. It is the kind of car that takes you back in time, making you feel quite disoriented. We have hired it to film some of the scenes on the route from Mumbai to Nasik and the five of us are divided between the jeep and the Ambassador. Each car has its own driver because you need to know the roads well to be able to drive in India. Anna explains that she has just spoken to Margaret. They have found her – they have found my sister! Nirmala will be waiting for us in Nasik with all the details. Most important of all, my sister remembers me!

I cry with emotion inside the car which is parked by the side of a bridge. Emotions: fear and nervousness. A very long train goes by, loaded with people, and I remain mesmerised, watching it until it disappears in the distance. Usha. My sister is called Usha. She is alive and she remembers me!

I arrive in Nasik for the second time as an adult, knowing a little better where I am going. I had been happy to think that I was born here and had told the story many times. I had learned that the Hindu epic of Rama and Sita took place here and that the sacred waters of the river Godavari are as holy as the waters of the Ganges. Here too, they free the spirits of the dead by casting their ashes onto the water. Now it seems that I had the whole story wrong; Nasik is not the town where I come from, although I feel as if I am from here. I would like to be from here. For me, Nasik will always be the place where my life began.

Leaving everything we don't need at the hotel on the outskirts of town, the entire team climbs into the jeep and we drive in towards the centre, to the *ghats* leading down to the river. On either side of the road there are countless mechanics' workshops, shops selling tyres for cars and lorries and modern blocks of flats. A sign announces that we are about to cross the Godavari Bridge. Another bids us welcome to the sacred city in English. Completely indifferent to the traffic, a cow crosses the road. I see the river in the distance and we quickly draw near to park very close to the *ghats*, or stone steps. There are clothes hanging out to dry on the balconies of the houses nearby. I notice two women dressed in orange saris talking, standing in the entrance to a house.

We spend the afternoon filming, surrounded by people who watch me with curiosity without knowing who I am or why a camera is following me from a distance.
The *ghats* are full of women washing clothes which they beat against the earth with a kind of wooden bat. The river water is dirty and I don't see how the saris manage

157

to come out clean. There is a constant movement of women carrying aluminium washbasins on their heads, coming and going from the house to the river, their ankle bracelets jangling as they walk. There is a festive air. The *ghats* are surrounded by little temples and the landscape is a picture postcard. While the women are washing clothes and talking happily amongst themselves, some children slip away to play naked in the water. Further down, a group of teenagers earns a few rupees cleaning motorcycles and rickshaws. The cows wander about without any idea of where they are going in the midst of all this. The fruit and vegetable stalls are stretched out under plastic coverings along the banks of the water. You can buy anything along the roadside from the little stalls mounted on wooden carts: kitchen utensils, glass bracelets, shoes, cassettes with every kind of music.

Nasik is preparing itself for the celebration of Kumba Melah, a few days from now. They are expecting millions of people, including pilgrims, *saddhus* and tourists arriving from every corner of India. There are signs announcing it everywhere, and the most frequent question we are asked is whether we will be in Nasik when the Kumba Melah begins. It is one of the most popular pilgrimages in the world and is held periodically in different cities in India. Once every thirteen years it is the turn of Nasik and Trimbak, a nearby town. The year 2003 is special because of the alignment of the planets, especially the proximity of Mars to Earth. The Kumba Melah is celebrated throughout the whole year, but it is only in the very first days that the pilgrims arrive in such massive numbers.

At dusk, just before darkness falls, in that magical hour around seven in the evening, the bells of the Kala Ram Mandir temple can be heard, in honour of the god Ram. I walk over. The vendors selling necklaces of fresh flowers outside are trying to get rid of everything before the day ends. Necklaces of white flowers, orange, yellow, pink, red... I cross the threshold and enter the grounds. In the middle of the square yard there is a temple, with a main stone staircase and two on the side. I take off my shoes like everyone else before climbing the steps and leave my sandals next to all the others. There are a lot, in every shape and size. At the end of the little room in the temple is an image of Ram, with a black face. I walk up to the altar, following a family which has come to say their prayers and I do as they do: I pass my hands over the flame of a fire, take water from a bowl and pass it over my face, pass my hands backwards over my hair and dot my forehead with the red powder that is lying on a tray.

Sitting on the stone steps as I come out of the temple, in the last rays of daylight, I am approached by families, curious old women wanting to ask who I am and where I come from, in Marathi at first, until it becomes plain that I do not understand. Then a girl appears who speaks English and I manage to explain my story, of why I have come back to Nasik. I tell them that I know I was born nearby and that my parents were named Radhu and Shevbai Ghoderao. They all start speaking, things that I can't understand, talking among themselves. Radhu and Shevbai appear to be very common names in this area. I am pleased to hear how they pronounce them. How they say what could have been my surname, Ghoderao. Shevbai is pronounced 'Sheobai'. I shed a few tears. Two old ladies with affable looks embrace me and wish me luck in their own way – they ask the gods to protect and help me. The place, the moment, everything is very special. The people of Nasik who look at me as though I am one of them, come back to find my roots, asking among themselves if the names of my parents sound at all familiar, the way you would ask after a neighbour or an old acquaintance. The people look at me with affection. An affection which touches me deep inside.

❊

Now the moment seems to have arrived to try to reconstruct the story of the first six years of my life. I am nervous. I cross the garden of the Dev-Mata convent (pronounced 'Deo-Mata'), where I lived until I was three years old. I recall the place perfectly from my first visit, everything is the same except for the swing which was in the middle of the garden and is no longer there. It is drizzling. There are flowers everywhere and the garden is very well looked after. I ring the bell, and Nirmala, who was expecting me, comes out to meet me. We hug each other and are overcome by powerful feelings. Now more than ever, it is clear to me that Nirmala is one of the most important people in my life. No sooner are we inside than Nirmala goes into the chapel, just inside the entrance, and says a prayer aloud in a mixture of English and Spanish. I follow her in silence. She thanks God for letting her see me again, for my safe arrival, and asks that everything will go well for me and that I will find what it is I have come to look for. Afterwards, we sit at the table in the hall by the entrance, with three windows that look out onto the garden. Nirmala explains to me that, just as I asked, she has done everything she could to find out the beginning of my story with as much accuracy as possible.. She has asked someone to help us, a man whom she has great confidence in. I shall meet him soon.

Later on, while we are having tea in a small dining room that is used only by the nuns, Francis Waghmare arrives to tell me everything he has managed to find out. He is our personal detective. Francis Waghmare teaches Marathi to boys and girls from age nine to sixteen at the Saint Philomena school in Nasik, very close to Dev-Mata. His wife is a nurse at the hospital. They have a daughter, Aditi, and a son, Aditya, ten year-old twins. He is three years older than I am and he inspires a lot of confidence. He sits at the table next to the window with myself, Nirmala and Merlyn, the mother superior at Dev-Mata who also took care of me when I first arrived. She was very young and remembers me perfectly!

Francis stares straight into my eyes, as if he wants to know if I am really who I say I am, or else is trying to guess what I am thinking. He too is in an emotional state. I return his gaze and imagine that he can read my profound gratitude for someone who is about to hand me such an important part of my life. He tells me that he asked for a few days off work so that we could go around the villages on his Vespa looking for all the missing pieces of my childhood. With his cup full of tea he begins his story.

Radhu Ghoderao married a woman called Shevbai. They had a son and four daughters. When Shevbai died, Radhu married another woman much younger than him and of feeble health, named Sitabai. Her surname was Sansare, and Balhegaon-Nagda was the name of her village. They say that Sitabai was very pretty and that her family decided to marry her to a man who was older than her and already had children because of her poor health. No one else wanted her, she had serious heart troubles and asthma. They lived in Shaha, a small village some seventy kilometres from Nasik, where Radhu was from.

Despite her weak physical state, Sitabai bore two boys and three girls: The eldest was a girl called Matura; the two boys died very young; the fourth was a girl named Asha and the smallest one was called Usha. I was Usha. When Usha was three months old, Sitabai passed away. She was already very ill and the last birth was more than she could take.

Francis didn't manage to find out much about Matura, except that she died many years ago. What many people did remember, however, is that Radhu was suddenly left alone with one very young girl and a three month old baby. By coincidence, at the same time that Usha, which is to say I, was born, one of Radhu's daughters from his first marriage, Sakubai, who was almost the same age as Sitabai, also gave birth to a child. The boy was named Balu. Radhu went to see his daughter Sakubai to ask her if she could breast feed Usha to prevent her dying of malnutrition. So Usha's half-sister nursed her and her own son for several months. I was nursed by my half-sister! This went on until her husband's family began to look unfavourably on the fact that she was sharing her milk between the two babies. The boy took precedence and they pressured her not to nurse little Usha any longer.

Time went by and Radhu couldn't leave the house. He should have been working in the fields, but with two little girls, even with some help from family and friends, he could see no way out of his situation. They were very poor. Radhu worked his field with buffalo. These were hard years of long droughts and small harvests. And so it was that one day he went to the neighbouring village of Pathri and explained his case to the catechist, or religious teacher, who lived there. Muralidhar Sakharam Waghmare was known to be a very good person who was always helping people. He was also Francis's father, the same Francis who now was telling me this story which I had difficulty believing was actually my own, and which was not quite finished yet. I was swallowing my tea in gulps, trying to keep the knots in my stomach down.

Every Monday, Francis's father would receive a visit from a priest and a nun from Nasik who would bring medicines for the people from the villages in the area, hold Mass and help in any way they could. The priest was from Madrid and was called Martín de los Ríos. The nun was from Goa and was called Nirmala Dias. Francis's father told them of Radhu's little girl and asked them if they could help. Francis was not exactly sure how it happened but within three or four Mondays I was handed over to Nirmala and from that moment on the nuns took care of me.

Nirmala is listening to the story and nodding her head in agreement, as if suddenly the memory of all these images came back to her, but she says nothing and lets Francis continue.

Before leaving me, Radhu, my father, wanted to do one last thing: change the names of the two girls. Asha means hope and he decided that little Usha would need hope and luck in her life. Usha means sunrise, dawn, and is the goddess of morning. Asha was called Usha. And that was how I, Usha Ghoderao, became, one Monday in 1968 (or it might have been 1969), Asha. The name which has always been with me, giving me strength.

It is difficult to describe what I feel as I try to take in what I have just been told. Nirmala is remembering it all and is as moved as I am. Until now this part of the story was half forgotten and confused in her mind. She has lived through the stories of so many girls! Tears are running down my face. But where is Usha?

'Yesterday I went to her house to see her,' Francis tells me, his face lighting up. 'And she would really like to see you. She has never forgotten you and she actually tried to find you, but without means or resources it was impossible.'

My sister is still called Asha. After our father, Radhu, decided to change our names, Asha continued to be called Asha, perhaps because she was aware of what her real name was and a girl who is aware of who she is can't be made to change her name easily, even if the grown-ups decide to do so.

Asha, the other Asha, is married and has four children. Tomorrow we can go and see her. My heart is beating. Tomorrow!

⚜

A nun comes into the dining room and breaks up the conversation looking very worried. There are three men outside who want to see Nirmala. One of them is the husband of my sister, who has come from Kolpewadi, a village about eighty kilometres from Nasik. The other two are his cousins who live in the town and decided to accompany him.

My brother-in-law – it is strange to think that I could call somebody that, someone whose name I don't even know – came all the way by bus on his own to see me, to know if I really exist, because he can't believe that his wife's sister has suddenly appeared just the way Francis explained it. Nirmala is concerned. She is worried they

will ask for money. In India, the Catholic nuns and
the convents are not very popular and have even been
attacked in some states. This puts them in a state of alert.
We go outside and find the three men, more frightened
than we are. Their eyes fill with tears to see me come
down the steps from the door. I exist. I am Usha, and
yes, tomorrow, if you have no objections, we will go to
Kolpewadi where the two sisters will be reunited.

Anna takes a picture of the three men, Nirmala, and
me. The two cousins insist on giving me their address so
that we can send them a copy. Asha's husband will return
to the village this evening. I feel sorry for him having to
make such a long trip, but he doesn't seem to mind. He
is as happy as he is incredulous.

When the three men leave, Francis explains that Asha's
husband is called Bikhaji Balaji Meherkhamb and he
works in a sugar cane factory in Kolpewadi. He and my
sister have two boys and two girls: Sheetal, who is twenty,
is now married and no longer lives with them; Savita,
seventeen years old, who is to marry soon; Bhausaheb
who is thirteen; and Rahul who is eleven.

Nirmala and Merlyn wish us much luck for tomorrow.
They are going through all this with as much intensity
as I am. Nirmala seems like a grandmother to me, like
a person who practically watched me being born. She
was the one who took the first steps towards giving me a
new life when Radhu asked her to help them. It is easier
for me now to understand the work of these women and
what Nirmala's role was in my adoption. Perhaps because

of her shyness and her sweetness, I was unable to realise just how much Nirmala had done for me the first time I was here. Nirmala was one of the first people who cared for me once my father left me with her, and it has been proven that in the process of growing as a person the most important thing is the affection you receive when you are very little. She was also the one who decided that I could not stay in Nasik forever. In those days there weren't that many children at Dev-Mata. I can only remember Johnny, my playmate. Nirmala says that he is dead. He was adopted by an Indian family and he died years ago of an illness. Nowadays, Dev-Mata looks after more than eighty orphan girls of all ages and they have constructed a separate building for them, where they can sleep, eat, and have classes. I saw them and I played with them for a time. Laughing with the little girls of the villages around Nasik in the Dev-Mata gardens is the closest I can get to the early years of my childhood.

5

Daughters of
the Godavari

Our lives are dotted with special dates marked in our personal calendar like constellations. The 28th of June 2003 is just such a date: I shall meet my biological sister, Asha, with whom I imagine I have a lot in common, but then again, perhaps not.

Now I wish I could meet someone who has been through a smiliar experience and could explain to me what to do in this situation, what I am supposed to say, whether it is normal to feel this mixture of fear and excitement, of wanting it to be happening and not wanting it at the same time.

We head towards Kolpewadi. Two hours in the white Toyota thrown about by all the bumps in a badly covered asphalt road that should be two lanes but often converts to four. There are eight of us squeezed together in the jeep including the driver, Akaram, who is driving as fast as he can. Apart from Francis, we are also accompanied by Vinod Bedarkar, a journalist on the local paper, *Sakal*, which is published in Marathi and can be bought all over the state of Maharashtra. He wants to write an article about what happens today. He is tall and slim, with a moustache and a dark gaze. Seated in the back of the car, in among all the film equipment, he watches us avidly without understanding what we are saying. My nerves are shattered; I have only managed to get a couple of hours sleep.

Francis explains to us that the district of Nasik encompasses fifteen *talukas*, which is the name given to the area surrounding each village. There are a lot of fields on either side of the road. It is the time for ploughing and the men work the land, helped by bulls or emaciated cows. Women wearing lively coloured saris, which contrast with the dull brown hues of the earth, carry water in big aluminium jars on their heads or against their sides. They pass through the flat landscape with their very elegant way of walking. It is a grey day with a lot of clouds, but the air is warm and humid. We pass by Pangri, a village cut through by the road. There is a

Hindu procession. The orange robes dominate the scene as the people follow along behind the little altar, carrying flags and garlands of flowers. We move on between herds of goats, dogs, motorcycles, houses without roofs, very modest restaurants and bars at the roadside with large signs for Fanta or Coca-Cola which contrast with the semi-desert of the landscape. Nearly all the men in the villages of this *taluka* wear a *Gandhi topi*, a white hat like an old-fashioned sailor's cap. it is the same white as the *salwar kameez* they are wearing.

We stop at a crossroads and Francis indicates a small road which leads off to the left, towards Shaha, the village where I was born. Asha ended up living just a few kilometres from our village while I was thousands of kilometres away. I examine the landscape as the car stops by the side of the road. It is all very flat. The earth is a certain shade of brown and the trees have peculiar shapes. They are called *babhool* and they belong to the acacia family. Shaha. I repeat the name of my village trying to discover what the sound evokes in me. The contradictions continue. On the one hand I feel an intense emotion, and on other, complete indifference. With my gaze fixed on the direction of the little road that leads to Shaha, I ask myself whether it really matters whether I was born in Shaha, Nasik or any other spot in the world. Why does it matter to so many people to know where we are from rather than who we are? I don't have an answer.

Pathri, Francis's village, is where my natural father, Radhu Ghoderao, handed me to Nirmala and Martín de los Ríos so they could give me a better life than the one he could offer me. At the entrance to the village, on a road that looks important but is not asphalted, we stop to shoot some film and an immense crowd, most of them boys and men, surround us curiously. It is not at all normal for a car like ours to turn up full of strangers. Some of the men recognise Francis (a school colleague, a neighbour) and ask insistently who we are. They press in so closely that we cannot move and until he tells them everything they want to know they will not step back and allow us a little air. All the roads in the village are made of earth. The houses are very small, and are also the colour of earth.

We arrive at the stone house where Francis lived as a child, which was also a dispensary for handing out medicines to the needy. He has forgotten the keys, which his mother still keeps in Nasik, so we can't go inside. No one lives there any more. We sit together on the stones at the entrance. It moves me to think that this is the house where my second life began, the one I have now. If my father had not brought me here I would have lived an entirely different life. Francis tells me that he had not really thought about this episode in his family history until Nirmala asked him to 'investigate' for me. Now, with the two of us sitting on the stones of the catechist's house, I silently observe the houses along the road in front of me, a landscape that we shared when we were young. Francis says that practically nothing has changed in more than thirty years. Some women sitting on the ground are washing aluminium jars; a piglet crosses the road looking for something to eat. Neither they nor I make any move to approach one another. There are only women, and the women, as opposed to the men we met at the entrance to the village, observe everything discreetly from a distance. Alongside Francis's house is a little temple that looks as though it has been abandoned. It exudes tranquillity. In this house I began my journey towards a new life, the first step towards Barcelona.

We arrive in Kolpewadi by means of a bridge which crosses the river, where the women are washing clothes. On the outskirts are some houses, very simple, most of the walls made of mud, some of them brick. There are cows, with their long, pointed horns, tethered to wooden carts with big wheels parked in the middle of the yards. There are also some cars, motorcycles and bicycles to be seen. Francis guides us to the neighbourhood of Kalgaon-Thadi, on the edge of Kolpewadi, and we park the jeep at the top of the road, still some way off from my sister's house. A large group of men and boys gathers around us, hardly allowing us to open the doors to get out of the car. It starts to rain. My nerves are on edge and I no longer know what I feel.

What should I say to my sister? What do you say to a sister whom you haven't seen for so many years? What do you say to a sister from whom you have been separated by seas and deserts, beliefs and languages, cultures and experiences? And she – will she be as nervous as I am?

I walk down to her house along the uncovered road, accompanied by Francis and the journalist from the paper *Sakal*. A group of men dressed in white, with the same old-fashioned sailor's cap, and children in blue school uniforms follow us doggedly down the street making a great racket. It looks like a procession. We pass a fountain. There are cows everywhere, and hens running back and forth. A strange silence comes as all of a sudden the rain stops, as if it too wants to observe what is happening.

❄❄

My sister's house is very typical for a normal village family, the family of a man who works in a sugar cane factory. These houses are called *vasti*. My sister's is a square construction of brick with a corrugated Uralite sheet roof and a little porch with plastic chairs. At the entrance are two buffalos with very long horns and young calves, all a very dark grey, tied to the little stable... And there is Asha. Dressed in a pink sari, slim like me, with the same dark gaze as me, with her hair tied up. And as emotional as I am. Francis introduces us. It is obvious that even he, who was so sure of himself up until this point, has no idea how to act or what to say.

Asha and I embrace. We laugh and cry, but speaking is impossible. I don't know enough Marathi, which is the only language she speaks. It all seems to happen in slow motion. Bikhaji, her husband, is here. He looks much happier than he did yesterday. His wife is happy and so is he. Today is a big day for the Meherkhamb family.

Sheetal, my eldest niece, who is married and lives in another village, couldn't come, but the other three are here. They are very happy to see me. We sit on the porch on the red plastic chairs, and Francis acts as our interpreter. Now it is as if not just the rain has stopped, but time also. Completely.

We sit side by side, the two Ashas, holding hands. We look at one another without saying anything; all we can do is cry. I have never looked at anyone this way, wanting to see myself reflected in her eyes, knowing that it is possible that I am still in there, that my image has remained imprinted in her mind all these years. Asha also looks at me with an expression of curiosity, emotion and surprise. How had she imagined me? What idea did she have of me? What is the last image of me she can recall?

It is clear that she is my big sister, and she treats me as such. She dries my tears with her sari and tells me things to console me which I don't understand. This intimacy is limited as almost the entire village is watching. I understand that this could not be avoided, but I would prefer not to have this spectacle in Kalgaon-Thadi. The neighbours, mostly men and boys, form an uncontrolled mass of people who encircle the house and climb the posts of the small cattle stable. It is strange that it doesn't collapse under them. The women are all gathered together on one side of the house, further away. Out of the corner of my eyes I watch them and see that some of them are so moved that they are passing handkerchiefs from one to the other. Suddenly the entire village is living these moments as though they are part of their own story. They laugh and cry with us. Feelings can also be experienced communally. They feel that Asha's story is also their own.

Asha shows me her house, with Francis translating everything she tells me. There is only one room, its walls painted a very light green. A garland of orange flowers hanging over the door bids us welcome. It is a small rectangular room, about twelve square metres, not much more, with a bed pushed into one corner next to the window by the entrance, and one piece of furniture (a wardrobe with doors). There are no objects or appliances of any kind, only a Chinese paper lantern hanging from the ceiling, a picture of Jesus and a wooden clothes horse with a few things hanging on it. On one of the walls three posters of landscapes have been stuck up along with another of the English alphabet for children. Opposite the entrance there is another door which leads to the latrines and the area which is used for washing oneself. The kitchen is dark with only one tiny window. A washbasin, a stove, some pots with flour, tea, spices, aluminium plates... There is only one light-bulb in the whole house and to put it on my niece, Savita, has to climb up on one of the red plastic chairs from the porch to hand the electric cable, which is rolled up in a crack in the wall, to her father so that he can fix it to the end of a fork-shaped stick and then cross the road to connect it inside another house. The windows have bars on them but no glass. Savita and the two children sleep on mats on the floor while Asha and Bikhaji sleep on the bed. They probably have to do their homework from school on the floor as well and that is also where they amuse themselves when it is raining and where they all eat together. I find it difficult to picture scenes from their daily life. Everything is so spartan and reduced to the minimum that it is difficult to describe.

Asha goes into the kitchen with two other women who help her to fry a kind of noodle made of potato paste and some fritters made of onion mixed with another ingredient that I don't know. She moves around the kitchen energetically, talking non-stop with her friends. The way she puts the fritters into the boiling oil is firm and determined. She seems to be the centre of this household and I am happy to hear her talking to the others. We eat what comes out of the kitchen served on aluminium trays, all seated on the floor between the wardrobe and the bed, and surrounded by dozens of people trying to enter the house, or else watching us from the doors and windows, all jostling one another. We must really make quite a spectacle. I feel like a wild animal in a zoo. We have to ask them to move back a bit from the two doors because we don't have enough air to breathe! It is very hot and the humidity makes it even more intense. Asha takes a fritter and puts it in my mouth, without warning and without giving me a chance to respond. Another fritter, a biscuit... Later on, they explain to me that this gesture of giving food to someone is a sign of affection.

My two little nephews, Bausaheb and Rahul, look a lot like me – so much so that someone remarks that they could easily be my own children. Physically they resemble me more than they resemble their mother, but they are also like me in the way they look and speak, and in certain gestures. I am quite conscious of this. It is clear that we are family, they too can see it and they are happy. They are very sweet and never stop smiling and going in and out of the house to chat to their neighbourhood friends and classmates outside. All the children are wearing their blue uniforms from the school. My nephews seem to be very intelligent and know perfectly well who I am and why I have come to their house to visit. Despite the scarce resources of my sister's family, the boys are very passionate about their studies. They observe everything, without letting a single detail escape, and they repeat all the phrases they know how to say in English as if they are trying to demonstrate that they can speak and we can understand each other correctly.

My niece, Savita, has not stopped smiling ever since we met. She is very affectionate and is attentive to everything. She helps her mother to bring one more chair here, another cup of tea there, and with everything else that is going on.

I have always imagined what it would be like to meet my natural family and often wondered if they would be like me. I always thought we would have nothing in common, that my Mediterranean gestures, the way I spoke, picked up from my adoptive parents, the education I received in Barcelona, all of this would distance me from those with whom I shared a mother, a father, grandparents and other ancestors. I have always defended the idea of the adoptive family and the idea that the adopted culture is the one which leaves its mark. But now I don't know what to think. Despite the fact that there are more things that separate us than bind us together, and despite the fact of having to speak through an interpreter, which makes good communication impossible, I still feel that in some way I am at home here.

But I am also very aware that it would be impossible for me to live here. I am sorry to have to acknowledge this. I look at them, Asha, her husband, their children, knowing for certain that they are my family and that they would give everything for me. Everything and more, even though I am still a total stranger to them. We know nothing about one another, but despite everything we are bound by very strong feelings. I wish so much that my parents could suddenly appear from Barcelona to witness everything that I am experiencing.

My two young nephews insist, one after the other, that we take pictures of all three of us together, lots of photos. I live each scene as if it were a film.

Before I have really come to terms with the vast magnitude of it all I begin to think of what I could do for them. A school, a medical dispensary for the village, a cultural centre. Just a little bit of economic help could make an enormous difference to Kolpewadi and the idea makes me feel both happy and a little uneasy. It would take a lot of work to keep track of it from a distance, to make sure it was working properly. I would like to take my two young nephews with me today, hidden in my baggage, halfway around the world to show them where I live... For a moment I imagine Asha in my house, cooking, looking at my photo-albums, and introducing her to my parents.

And while all these ideas are turning over in my head, I also feel that I am thinking of helping them in the most typical Western terms which makes me feel a twinge of embarrassment. A school? They already have one! A medical dispensary, a cultural centre... Perhaps they don't need any of that! Surely they would just prefer me to come and visit them more often. Maybe they would be uncomfortable if Asha's sister, whose life led her to Europe, and who now has a life that is unattainable for them, turned around and started changing the whole village. It has to be thought over carefully. What I do know is that finding my sister has not been a simple thing and that right now a huge question mark hangs over whatever might come out of this, for her as much as for me.

❧❧

'I prayed a lot to be able to find you, and I knew that I would find you, that one day I would see you again.' Asha tells me this through Francis on the way to Shaha, the village where we were both born. 'There are so many things I would like to tell you!' The language really gets in the way. She speaks Marathi with some dialectical differences. They tell me that normally she talks a lot and that I shouldn't think she is shy or reserved, just that at the moment she can't say everything she would like to. 'What a shame you don't speak Marathi!' Yes, it is a shame. I got over that particular disappointment the first time I came back to India, when I longed to be able to understand what had been my language. Children can entirely erase their native language in less than six months if no one speaks it to them, or if they don't hear it spoken anywhere. When those same children grow up, however, they might possess a greater facility for learning that forgotten language, because the sounds are left somewhere in their memory. I would like to study Marathi some day, and return to Kolpewadi and be able to have a conversation with my sister without an interpreter of any kind. Francis is a perfect translator, the best interpreter we could possibly have. He never stops talking, in one language or another. He too, is a part of our story and these moments are very intense for him. Even before I ask, he comes over to explain things that he thinks are important, repeating them as many times as it takes for me to understand. His accent in English is a little difficult for me to understand and he has to work hard to allow both Asha and myself to express ourselves through him.

Asha and I are sitting in the front of the jeep, with Akaram driving in the direction of Shaha. In the back seat are Jordi,

Francis and the journalist. At the very back, bouncing and laughing among the cameras and bags, are Mikele, Anna and Grau. There is no end to the holes in the road.

When we were leaving Kalgaon-Thadi to go to Shaha, Asha's husband wanted to come with us, but there wasn't room. He stayed behind. I think he is a little worried that we will take Asha away!

We drive along a narrow, winding road. Three children are squatting by the side of the road, relieving themselves. It seems to be the most entertaining place to take care of such necessities, chatting and watching the cars, carts and bicycles going by. All three of them wave enthusiastically as we go by, without getting up, and with their pants down.

❄

I imagine Radhu ploughing the field just like the men we can see through the window of the jeep, dressed in white, working the dark and dusty earth. We pass through villages with houses made of mud with straw roofs and small houses made of brick, square, recently constructed. I note every detail of the landscape, solitary, dry, the shape of the trees... We leave the small road and turn on to the main road, which is a little better than the one which leads from Shirdi (a town where there is a big Sai Baba temple) to Nasik. Asha and I spend a good deal of the journey holding hands, as though we don't want to experience what we are seeing separately. We are both very emotional on the way to Shaha. It is as if by holding hands we can transmit what each of us is feeling. There are moments in life when words are not necessary.

Shaha belongs to the *taluka* of Sinnar, a very poor and dry zone where cultivation is not easy. Asha tells me that she goes there often, every couple of months or so to visit all the family who live there, at least the ones she is in contact with. We turn onto another road. This is very narrow and there is almost no asphalt left on it. The journey seems very long to me, the monotony of the untamed landscape, which is lovely, makes me nervous instead of relaxing me. When I am least expecting it we arrive at Shaha. We pass through the length of the village because it turns out that we were born in a place called Chari Kramanka Athara, which can be translated as Shaha's Channel Number 18, a kind of conduit that brings water from the Godavari. We are daughters of the Godavari.

We pass a red tractor with a couple who wave and smile at us. On either side of the road there are fields of corn, cows, herds of goats... Now we are there. We enter the neighbourhood, or quarter, or whatever they call it on the outskirts of Shaha. Channel Number 18 and the asphalt disappears completely. Two boys on bicycles escort us and show us the way. It is quite unusual for a car full of so many foreigners to turn up in Shaha.

We get out of the car. There are a few mud houses with straw roofs, cows tethered to the stables and ploughed fields. The ground is hot. A warm breeze is blowing. It is silent. Women dressed in saris appear, then boys and men. I don't know where they come from because the village looks half-abandoned and the houses are small. Asha seems to know almost everyone and she presents me to them, one by one, and they all look at me as though hypnotised. I try to imagine what Asha must feel, presenting her sister to the people of the village where we were born, decades after that same sister had vanished from sight. I feel a knot in my stomach and wonder if I am not dreaming all of this.

❦

We hold hands and we walk up to a field from which you can see the house where I was born. There, between those walls and that straw roof which cuts across the horizon, we lived together as children. Asha, less than forty years ago and me, Usha, about thirty five. Now I am in doubt about my age, about the date of my birth, but it doesn't matter. I am not interested in verifying it, and besides, it would be quite impossible to find anyone who could actually remember the exact date when Sitabai gave birth to little Usha. Asha suggests that we walk over to what used to be our house, across the fields, but the fatigue is getting to me now and I have no energy left. Having not slept for more than two hours and with all the accumulated emotion I am incapable of taking one more step. For the moment I am quite happy just to look at it from a distance.

And so, many years after having left Shaha, the two Ashas, one from the West and one from the East, stand hand in hand looking out across the fields at the horizon, listening to the sound of the wind in the trees. In the distance two men dressed in white are ploughing the fields, the horns of their cows are painted orange and turquoise blue. Our father, Radhu, must have done the same thing so many times! The ashes of our mother, Sitabai, are spread on the fields we are looking at, perhaps in the field that we are standing on now. There is nothing to indicate the exact spot. She died when I was three months old. I repeat to myself everything that I have discovered up until now, to fix it firmly in my memory. Sitabai. Sita. My mother had the name of a goddess! This is the name of my origins. I am wearing sandals and I can feel the heat of the earth through my feet. I think of Sitabai and I imagine her watching us, Asha and me together. United forever.

⁂

The people of Shaha watch us and I recognise myself in many of their faces. Some of them have the same blood as I do and they have a similar genetic make-up, but there is so much that separates us! They introduce me to the wife of our half-brother (the son of Radhu and Shevbai) and two of her children. One of them looks like me, like my young nephews, Asha's sons. It is obvious that we belong to the same family. I recognise myself in the faces that I see around me, in the faces of the people of Kolpewadi and Shaha. They too recognise me as a member of their family. So many familiar faces, what a strange sensation! I, who have always been so different from everyone else! Anna and Mikele are joking, 'Look, there's another Miró!' They are my people without actually being my people, because we share nothing but our physical appearance. I suppose you have to experience it to understand.

We retrace our journey to return to Kolpewadi. Asha's husband's face lights up when he sees us arrive, as do those of Savita, Bausaheb and Rahul. They say that it is a shame we have to go back to Nasik so soon, today, and that I have to come back again soon with more time to spare, that there are a lot of people who want to see me, cousins, the children of cousins, uncles... The Meherkhamb house is still full of people, neighbours of every age curious to know more about the story.

I ask myself if I could last very long in the little house in that part of Kalgaon-Thadi, and once again I come to the conclusion that I am completely Western, in the worst sense of the word. I have become used to all the modern conveniences and would now be incapable of sleeping on the ground in the little room of the Meherkhamb house with everyone around me, literally living on top of one another with no privacy, listening to everyone breathing, one coughing, another having a nightmare. I might be able to spend a day there, but I have to admit that it would be no more than that. And I wouldn't even know where to begin washing myself in their bathroom where there wouldn't be room for even half of my soaps and creams. I think that I would die of hunger, too, because I find it difficult to eat Indian food, the spices, everything that I am not familiar with. Getting used to the water, too, which I know it's better not to drink because our bodies are not used to it (despite taking precautions, I have suffered the effects since the first day), and all the tea with milk they drink at any hour of the day and which I am not too keen on unless they add a disproportionate amount of sugar... I know that I would have a difficult time of it, and I am ashamed to admit it, but that is the way it is.

Asha and Savita show me family photos and the two younger ones help to comment as well. This is the scene that really brings us together, more than anything else that has happened since I arrived. The scene seems familiar and comfortable to all of us. The language of photographs is universal: sitting on the porch of a house passing pictures around of everything and nothing, a performance at the children's school, a fancy dress party, an excursion to a temple... Now I really do feel at home, part of the family. And they do, too. I would like to stretch this moment out to its limits. I would like to come back loaded down with my photos to explain in images everything that I have been through, from when they left me with the nuns until now. Perhaps that is what I should do soon.

Asha, the little girl who, with no say in the matter, suddenly found herself without her little sister, deserves an explanation. She deserves an answer from me to all of her questions, and since I cannot explain in words, it seems like a good idea to try with pictures. And I, too, have a lot of questions that I would like to have the time to put to her. We have enough on our hands today just taking in all of these new things.

They have called the village photographer and the family photo session begins. One after another they file onto the porch to be immortalised by my side.

Asha gives me two photographs from her collection to take back with me to Barcelona so as not to forget her, and a *salwar khameez* for me and another one for Anna. A group of neighbours have come into the house. Prodding and poking us, they insist, in between laughs and comments that we don't understand, on leading us into the kitchen where they strip us down half-naked and we wind up wearing the *salwar khameez* which makes us sweat even more. The language of clothes and women getting dressed up is universal.

❧❦

The moment to leave has arrived. Asha is crying; she walks to the jeep with me holding my hand. Each second is like an eternity. Once inside the car, after having hugged and kissed and said goodbye without words, she firmly takes my face between her two hands and then raps her knuckles on either side of her head. She repeats the very quick, precise gesture a couple of times. Savita says farewell in the same way, imitating the blessings of her mother. I wonder what exactly it means.

I will always remember Asha's open hand against the glass of the car window and her eyes filled with tears looking at me. Eyes bathed with sadness which I couldn't bear to see. Seeing her only makes me think of the little Asha, the Asha who lost her sister thirty years ago. I don't want this to be the last image I have of her. I want to see her again. We shall have to invent some way of communicating, but we can't let several more decades pass us by without knowing anything about each other. I ask Francis to tell her once more that I shall be back, that I will never forget her, that I will send news through him and she can send me news also. The whole village is there to wave goodbye. Some boys run along behind the car when it starts to move. I can't look back any more, I too am crying.

The fact of being told how alike we are as sisters makes me think of a person leading a kind of double life. Like the two faces of the moon, of a coin, of a reflection in a mirror. The Asha who lives in Kolpewadi could be the Asha who lives in Barcelona. I could be the other Asha. If Radhu had decided that it was more difficult to take care of a young child than a baby, I would have had another life, probably very similar to the one that Asha is living.

So similar that it might have been the same. By now I might have four children and a husband like Bikhaji. And the life of Asha might have been very similar to mine. Might she have been adopted by my parents? Could she have been the Catalan one and I the one who spoke only a dialect of Marathi? Or might she have been Swedish, or Italian, or French? The questions are endless and there are no possible answers.

In all stories of adoption there is an element of magic, of fate, of a predestined path, of choice, depending on each person's individual faith, which makes everyone unique and special. Today, for the first time, I have come close to seeing what my life might have been like had my father not handed me over to be adopted. I have come very close, so close that I could actually see myself living there. Asha means hope and perhaps my sister held on to her name in order to preserve the hope that she too needed.

Once back in Nasik, we say goodbye to Francis and his friend the journalist, who has to write his article straight away so that it can be published tomorrow. Francis has been more help than I could have imagined and I shall always be grateful to him for that.

We are once again in the Dev-Mata convent, crossing the garden which seems like an oasis of peace to me. Nirmala and Merlyn welcome us happily, having been waiting with great impatience to hear about everything that happened in Kolpewadi, with no detail spared. They have prepared tea for us and a cake which they made this afternoon. Nirmala is happy because she can see that I am happy, even though I am also very tired. Now she understands how important it was for me to reconstruct my past.

⁂

We go to the Church of Saint Anne, which is very close to the convent, the church where I was baptised. Nirmala and Merlyn go with us. The new chaplain – who when we arrive is playing football in the yard, casually dressed, with a group of children – hands us the registry book in which my certificate of baptism is noted, a big book with an antique look about it. It is the same book I saw a few years ago, when I last visited this place. That time I was content to settle for Father Prakaast, who looked after the chapel in those days, copying out all the information. Not this time. Now, I go through the old, yellowed pages written in English script with faded ink and my finger goes back over every entry. Number of baptism: 776. Date: 7th of May, 1969. Name: Asha Maria. Date of Birth: 7th November, 1967. Father's Name: Radhu Kasinath Ghoderao. Mother's Name: Shevbai Ghoderao.

And I stop there. Why put Shevbai's name when she was not my mother? It turns out that in those days and in that kind of register they only recorded the name of the first wife, who was the official wife, the only one that counted. Which is why Sitabai, my biological mother, doesn't appear anywhere! I still recall the emotion I felt the first time I read the name Shevbai, thinking that it was the name of the woman who gave birth to me. During the last few years I even thought that if I should ever have a natural daughter, I would call her Shevbai. Now I know that it wasn't Shevbai who gave life to me, though she did give life to my elder half-sister, Sakubai, who nursed me when my mother died. In some way I am also grateful to her and she also forms part of my genealogical tree, as unusual and full of curiosities as it is.

I continue reading the baptism certificate. Place of Birth: Shaha. I feel a tingle of excitement. All the pieces fit! If in 1995 I had insisted on reading this page of the registry book myself, I would not have spent all these years thinking that I had been born in Nasik. I finish going through the entries on the page. Father's profession: Farmer. Godparents: Stanislaus Gonzalves (Nirmala explains that he was the father of Meena, one of the Dev-Mata nuns) and Maria Angela Dias (Nirmala's cousin). Chaplain: Martín de los Ríos. I breathe easily. It looks like everything makes sense now, that it has all taken its final shape, that there is no longer room for any more confusion.

The day is coming to an end and I embrace Nirmala for the last time. She is crying. We are all crying. I don't know what to say to her. I don't know if I have told her everything I want to say, everything I have felt. I don't know if I can find the words to thank her for having asked Francis to find out everything he could about my past, for having helped me to find my sister. More than anything else, though, for having accepted the request made by Radhu and Francis's father when I was a baby, one day towards the end of the 1960s. For having looked after me when I was little, during the years at Dev-Mata, and later for having insisted on transferring me to Regina Pacis in Mumbai so that I could receive an education. I suppose that she must have realised that sending me to Mumbai would increase my chances of having a better future. How many important things have happened in my life thanks to the woman who I am now embracing!

Nirmala stays there with Merlyn but tomorrow will return to Mumbai, where she now lives most of the time. She is worried about her health but she is strong and I hope to visit her many more times. I leave the Dev-Mata grounds through the iron gate, my face covered in tears and with a profound sense of gratitude, knowing that I shall always have a home here; Merlyn, who is now in charge of the convent, told me this seriously, and I believe her.

That evening, when we arrive at the hotel outside Nasik, they ask me at the reception if I am Asha Ghoderao. It is the first time anyone has asked me that question and I am quite struck by it. 'Yes, I am. Why?' One of the receptionists hands me a sheet they use for noting down messages for their guests. Someone has called asking for Asha Ghoderao. From that moment on I receive a number of phone-calls from cousins and relatives of every kind living in Nasik who have found out that I am staying in this hotel. They have heard all kinds of details about the meeting between the two Ashas... Since their English is as precarious as mine, the conversations can't really get too involved. One of them gives me his e-mail address and asks me to write to him, another asks me to come to their house to meet all of their family... I tell them all that I have to leave for Mumbai soon and that from there I am flying back to Barcelona. They don't understand. If I have now managed to find my family, why am I going back to Barcelona? I realise that for many of them it seems a great pity to be living so far away from India, while others think I am very lucky. I continue to be torn by contradictory feelings: Now that I know I am from here originally, I would like to understand the way of life in this country a little better, but I am so European that it would be very difficult for me to adapt.

I didn't dream it all. I wake up in Nasik and realise that everything that happened yesterday was real. Asha and Usha, the two Ashas. We managed to meet again years after our paths in life were separated. The hotel staff greet me with a special smile: the newspaper *Sakal* has published Vinod Bedarkar's article with a colour photograph of myself and Asha on the front page. Thousands of readers all over the state of Maharashtra are now acquainted with our story. While the article about our reunion circulates around Maharashtra, the English language press continues to concern itself with talk about Bollywood cinema and its latest hits, about the disputes between Muslims and Hindus over the construction of a temple, the spectacular growth of the class of wealthy Indians, the death of hundreds of people in a terrible accident on the night train between Karwar and Mumbai, the consequences of the invasion of Iraq in March – 'invasion' is the word they use. Between the international news and the most modern photographs there are two pages full of parents looking for the ideal husband or wife for their sons and daughters. It is surprising to note that the most sought after are the NRIs (Non-Resident Indians), Indians who live abroad. India is a country of great contrasts, with some extremely rich and Westernised people living only a few metres from people who have practically nothing. A country which is advancing, which has some great intellectuals, the largest cinema industry in the world, but which, in contrast, continues to be ruled by ancestral customs such as marriages arranged by the parents.

I put aside all the other papers and sit with *Sakal* in my hands. It gives me a strange feeling to see the photograph of me and my sister on the front page. I ask them to translate the text and find it funny to hear the story being told once more.

After breakfast I take a walk around the centre of Nasik and use the opportunity to buy several copies of *Sakal* from a small news-stand on the street. I pass a big elephant and give it a few coins, which it takes with its trunk and hands up to its owner sitting on top. The diversions of Sunday morning on the streets of this town. I walk across the bridges and down the narrow streets with more peace of mind than ever, at ease, as if I were at home. Nasik could have been my hometown, and in fact it is my town.

6

Sitabai And Sakabai

Several days have gone by since I was reunited with my sister. I have lost all sense of time, it seems as though it was ages ago. In India, time feels different, as if it passes more slowly. I still don't know quite what I feel, it's very difficult to describe. I still have so many questions to put to Asha! It all happened very quickly and I need to see her again. I want to know more about her. And I suppose that she has even more questions for me.

Taking advantage of being able to escape from filming, I ask Francis to help me a little more. I need him to act as an interpreter and I want to get to the bottom of my story, to find the few remaining pieces in order to understand what happened to my family, what became of my parents. Francis doesn't hesitate for a second and asks the director of the school where he works for a day off so that we can go round the little villages that we need to visit. This time we go without the cameras, only Anna and myself in a hired jeep. The new driver is called Kumar.

We leave early in the morning on the road to Kolpewadi without anyone else finding out we were going. It is hot, and the car runs a slalom around the hundreds of holes in the road, avoiding lorries, bicycles and dogs. 'If we tell them we are coming and word spreads, there will be at least five hundred people waiting as we enter the village,' Francis assures me. 'Especially after the article in *Sakal*, which touched a lot of readers.' Which is why we are not saying anything. I am only hoping that Asha will be there!

While we are going over some of the anecdotes in my story, Francis tells me that Sakubai, the woman who nursed me when my mother died, one of my father's daughters from his first marriage to Shevbai, lives not far away from the place we are driving through. 'Is she still alive?' 'Oh yes, she certainly is,' he says, and it seems that she was quite upset the other day when she found out that I had suddenly turned up out of nowhere and had not gone to see her! My immediate instinct is to ask

Kumar to turn off on to the dust road that leads in the direction of Ujani, which is the name of the village where Sakubai lives.

We stop the jeep and Francis, Anna and I walk towards a solitary house with a straw roof and mud walls surrounded by fields. The silence is complete. Between the *bajra* plants in one field, which is a kind of maize but smaller, longer and thinner, I see an old man, dressed completely in white and cutting grasses. Francis tells me that he is Sakubai's husband. We go over to him. The man looks at us in surprise and waits. When Francis introduces us, his feelings overwhelm him. Close up his shirt and trousers are not as white as they appear at a distance. His skin is very dark, and he looks very old, though he could not be more than sixty. He is Hari Jagtap, my half-sister's husband.

Sakubai is not there. At first, it seems as though she has been admitted to the hospital in Shirdi with respiratory problems. Then it turns out that she is visiting one of her daughters in a village on the outskirts of Shirdi, because she has very bad asthma and needs treatment. Every day she goes to the hospital and she can't move around very much. Shirdi is not far off from where we are now. Since it is early and in India time seems to stop for me, we decide to go and see her. Another surprise visit. But Hari wants to come with us. He doesn't lock the house or take anything with him. He simply rolls down the sleeves of his shirt and is ready. Hari and I walk from his fields to the jeep parked on the dust road holding hands. He takes my hand. I feel the rough, dry skin of his hand, which a moment ago was touching grass and earth, against my hand and I know that this man feels something special for me.

Now we are going to go to Kolpewadi to see Asha and then take her with us to visit Sakubai. We talk all the way from Ujani to Kolpewadi. Francis translates non-stop all the questions and answers. Hari seems to have a very good memory and unravelling the twists and turns of a story that happened thirty five years ago seems to pose no problems for him. He remembers perfectly how his wife, Sakubai, nursed me at the same time as her son, Baly, who is the same age as me.

The jeep advances slowly along the road and with each jolt I fix every new image of my story inside me. Between one piece of the story and the next, Hari watches me from deep within the depths of his dark gaze.

I ask him what my father was like, what he remembers of him. He knows everything apparently, but he doesn't know where to begin. He tells me that my father had his own land, he wasn't rich but he had enough to feed the whole family. He had some cows and buffalo, and even a horse, which he used for getting around. Both he and my grandfather, Kasinath Ghoderao, loved horses very much. Ghoderao means horseman.

Radhu had five children by his first wife, Shevbai. Hari doesn't say it like that, because, like everyone else, he counts the boys separately from the girls. So Radhu had one son and four daughters. The sons are always mentioned first, even if they were born last. The boy was Janardan. The girls were Kamala, Vimal, Sakubai, and Yamuna. Janardan was the third and Sakubai was the fourth. He had inherited the land from the family and he worked it with his son. But Janardan became an alcoholic and didn't do all the work needed of him, and Radhu couldn't do all of it alone. Janardan started to sell off the land piece by piece until he had lost it all. According to Hari, my father died in Shaha, in the same house where my mother died. He also remembers Sitabai well. Her hair was lighter than mine and she was more than thirty years younger than my father. She was only twenty years old when they were married. Just as Francis did, Hari tells me that she had two sons and three daughters. Matura was the eldest. The two boys were named Dingar and Ananada and they died when they were little. Then came Asha and me.

We arrive at Kolpewadi. Along the river, under the bridge, there are once again many women washing clothes along with a lot of bicycles and small shops where tailors sit working at their black sewing machines, watching everyone that comes and goes from the village. I recognise every detail until we reach the street where the Meherkhambs live. It is not raining today and everything looks different. In the sunlight the unmetalled road doesn't look the same at all. There is little activity. It is an ordinary day and no one is expecting us.

Suddenly the silence is broken by cries of, '*Maushi! Maushi!*' Savita, my niece, is the first one I see and she runs to embrace me, laughing all the while. Her hands are wet because she has been doing housework, but despite this she is dressed in a yellow sari and looks very elegant. *Maushi* means 'aunt'.

She introduces my eldest neice, Sheetal, who arrived just yesterday with her daughters to spend a few days. Rahul is there too because he didn't go to school today. But the others are not there. Asha is in the field and Bikhaji is probably at work in the factory. Bausaheb is still at school. We sit on the red plastic chairs on the porch to wait. They have gone to fetch everyone. The neighbourhood women are appearing out of curiosity. They recognise us immediately and it amuses them greatly to see us again, just as it is does us to see them. Kalgaon-Thadi is not a neighbourhood that is used to receiving visitors of this kind. One of the neighbours takes the initiative and lights the fire on one side of the porch so as to heat up some milky tea while we are waiting.

Finally Asha and Bikhaji arrive on a motorbike. Asha is sitting side-saddle in a purple sari. We embrace in front of her house. She doesn't understand what I am doing here but it doesn't matter. She thought it would be a lot longer before we saw each other again! She is very happy. I take a good look at her, from top to bottom. My sister. It is difficult to imagine that she wears such a lovely sari to work in the fields. I am still surprised by the contrast between the elegance of the Indian women and their way of life.

After having tea and calming down a little, as well as gettting to know Asha's mother-in-law, and after having a long talk with my nephews – with Francis's indispensible help – Asha and her husband climb into the jeep with us and Hari. Together, we all drive back along the road to Shirdi to go and visit Sakubai. Asha and Bikhaji think it is a very good idea to go and see her.

Coming into the town, we pass the Sai Baba temple on our left and follow a small road towards the outskirts, to a place called Nandurkhi. Hari points out the house and we stop in front of it. It resembles Asha's house. It is small and made of brick with a corrugated roof and a cement floor. Sakubai and her daughter Suman come out to meet us, or rather to see what is going on, and who Hari is with. They don't make a big fuss; clearly we are a long way from Mediterranean customs. Here people seem to keep their feelings inside them rather than let them out. But the look in their eyes and the expressions on their faces say so much! Sakubai knows immediately who I am. The first thing she asks Francis is to translate that this visit is a great gift to her. She tells me this while holding my arms firmly in hers. She was very sad to hear that I had been to the Meherkhamb house in Kolpewadi and that she didn't have a chance to see me. Sakubai is probably much younger than she looks. She is wearing a white and pale pink sari with a purple blouse underneath, glasses and a lot of glass bracelets on each wrist. She has a very special way of looking at me. It is impossible that she could recognise me. The last time she saw me I was only a few months old. But I can sense that there are traces of the features of Sitabai and Radhu in my face, the faces of my parents. That is what she sees, that is what she is looking for in my expression. She is looking for them.

We sit down together on the only bed there is in the one room house, the two Ashas and Sakubai. Just as in Asha's house, there is nothing more than one bed pushed up against a barred window with no glass. Two white plastic chairs and a clothes hanger with some trousers, two shirts and a turquoise sari. Under the bed are some garlands of orange flowers alongside a pile of dried herbs. Hari sits on the floor, next to a dozen people who have come into the house. They are the sons and daughters of Hari and Sakubai. All of them are very quiet and respectful. Sakubai takes my hands, touches my face and looks at me. She cries and wipes the tears away underneath her glasses with her sari. 'When a woman has breast fed a child which is not her own she remembers it for ever.' This is one of the first things she says to me.

I begin to ask her about everything and she answers without pausing even for a second in finding the answers. It is all still very fresh in her memory, as though it happened yesterday. My mother, Sitabai, was her stepmother, the second wife of her father, Radhu, who was also my father. Normally, a man's children have to show respect to his new wife if he decides to marry again, both in their manner of addressing her and in their gestures. Sitabai had asked her and her other sisters not to bother with this show of respect. Sitabai was a few years younger than Sakubai and they became great friends. Such good friends that they ended up forgetting the family relationship that existed between them. They shared a lot of things, their worries, the birth of their children. They lived four kilometres apart, the distance that separates Shaha from Ujani. Sakubai had already had Balu when Sitabai's health began to fail. I had been born three months earlier.

The numbers don't really add up, the years don't fit. When it comes to calculating dates, all of us are guessing. Apart from Anna, I don't think anyone in this house really knows for certain which day and in which year they were actually born.

They took Sitabai to the doctor in Kolpewadi, but they had to bring her back home again. My mother was already very ill and nothing could be done for her. Her asthma problem had grown worse and she had great difficulty in breathing. She was suffocating. I will never know exactly what she had or what she died of. 'Sitabai died lying down on the bed in the house in Shaha, with her head resting on my skirt,' Sakubai tells me. 'I took care of her until the end.' We were all crying. Sakubai gives me her hand and I squeeze it. Thirty-five years later she is crying over the death of her friend, over the death of my mother, with such feeling that I am left speechless. Now I am the one who is drying her tears with her sari.

She takes off her glasses to let me do it. Between sobs, Sakubai tells me that one of the last times she went to see my mother they had had a long conversation. Sitabai told her that she knew she was going to die soon, and she asked her to take care of me, more than anything, not to let me die. 'I promised her that I would look after you, that you would not die.'

My mother was cremated on a pyre in the middle of one of the fields at Shaha, and her ashes were spread there. Asha tells her that we went there together a few days ago and that she showed me the place and the village.

On the day of Sitabai's death, Hari and Sakubai took me home with them to their house in Ujani. Radhu didn't know what to do with me, a baby only a few months old which needed to be nursed. Asha stayed there with the other, older siblings, while they carried me away on foot. Sakubai remembers having covered the four kilometres to Ujani with me on her back, nursing me from time to time. Hari carried little Balu, who was only two months old, in his arms. Sakubai had always known that when Sitabai died she would have to take care of her little ones. That was what Sitabai had asked her to do. They went to fetch Asha the following day, but she came and went between the two houses. They looked after me in that house for three months. By then they had discussed it with Radhu: Little Usha would stay there until they were sure she could survive, or else for good. Hari and Sakubai were much younger than Radhu and had more energy for taking care of children.

During the months I spent in her house as one of her children, Sakubai had the idea that it was like having twins and she would bring up Balu and myself as equals. Hari thought this was a very good idea and made sure that his wife ate as much as she could to keep up her strength so that she had enough milk for both babies. 'And I didn't let her work, I wanted you both to be taken good care of and didn't want her to get more tired than necessary,' Hari explained.

Then, one day, Hari's father, Kasinath Jagtap, forbade them to carry on raising me. He argued that Balu was not only their natural child, but was also a boy and therefore took precedence, and that Sakubai would not have enough milk for both and was risking the life of the baby who really mattered. Both Hari and Sakubai tried to persuade him otherwise, but they were unable to change his mind. Hari, looking into my face, explains to me in Marathi, which Francis translates for me, that his father was very strong, very dominant and very imposing. It wasn't possible to defy him. If it hadn't been for him, they would have adopted me and would have been my parents forever.

I am completely transfixed listening to this story. Sitting on the floor, at the foot of the bed on which we three sisters sit, Hari is crying inconsolably. I am the girl that could have been his daughter. In some ways I was his daughter for three months. When he stops crying he tells me firmly that he now thinks that, thanks to his father, I have had a better life. At the time they were very sad about having to let me go, but now he is content; 'If it hadn't been for my father you would be living like this, like us. I am sure you live much better and now I am happy.' Those are his words. It touches me that a man who lives so far outside the world, so disconnected from everything, illiterate, with no access to the news, no press, no television, could be so convinced that the life I have led has been better than that which he could have offered me. It touches me and makes me cry. Anything makes me cry now. It is a very powerful moment, experiencing what is happening to me, feeling what I am feeling now, as satisfying as it is hard to digest and absorb. I am sitting with the people who could have been my parents. I am closer than ever to my own mother. Sitabai and Sakubai resembled each other, they were practically the same age, they were friends. I want to remember forever the warmth and the feel of Sakubai's hand. She holds on to me and I feel as though I am living between the past they are telling me about, and the present. I feel out of time. Holding hands with my first adoptive mother, and with my sister, I feel at peace.

Carrying out the orders of Hari's father, they began to think about what to do with Usha, what to do with me. Radhu and Hari had heard of the catechist, Francis's father, in Pathri. The two of them went to see him alone. Radhu asked him for help with his two daughters, Asha and Usha. He wanted to give them to the chaplain and the nuns whom he knew went there every Monday, so that they could take care of them until they were grown up. Nobody could take care of them other than Hari and Sakubai, but they were being prevented from doing so. Francis's father listened to them. A few days later he went to Shaha to see the girls, Asha and me. Then he decided that to ask the nuns to take care of two girls would be too much. The older one, Asha, could now walk and eat by herself if need be. The little one, Usha, was only a few months old and was still very fragile. She needed feeding and caring for, otherwise she would die. He would tell them only about Usha, about me. The air could be cut with a knife, as we all listen to the story attentively. Neither Francis nor my sister knew about this and they are very surprised. Asha breaks the tension by saying that Francis's father took the right decision, otherwise she wouldn't have been able to live with Bikhaji! We all laugh. Bikhaji has been sitting in the corner all this time, listening to the story.

❧❧

The following Monday, Radhu and Hari returned to Pathri, only this time they had me in their arms. They met Martín de los Ríos and Nirmala. Yes, they were prepared to take care of me, but it wasn't all that simple.

They needed to have the permission of their superiors. When permission was granted, Sakubai and my father took the bus to Nasik. This was Sakubai's first visit to the city. She carried me in her arms all the way and my father carried Balu. Sakubai breastfed one and then the other. The journey took four hours. They passed through the wrought iron gates of Dev-Mata, the same gate which is there today, and they crossed the garden to the house. Sakubai clearly recalls the conversation Radhu had with Nirmala. Radhu wanted to leave me there only for a short time, just until I wasn't so fragile, until I could walk and eat rice and cereals. But Nirmala told him that would be impossible; if they left the child it would have to be for good. They both spent the night at the convent because it was already late. Then Radhu signed the papers, in a manner of speaking, that is, since he couldn't read or write. They arrived at an agreement with Nirmala: The nuns would bring little Usha back to the village once in a while and they would let them know how their little girl was doing.

Sakubai handed me over to Nirmala. It was she who actually did the physical act of placing me in the arms of another person. Afterwards, she, Radhu and little Balu went to catch the next bus back to the village.

'What else could be done but to leave you there? We were poor, we lived in the country, my father-in-law wouldn't allow me to raise you, and there was no one else to take care of you... Your mother had asked me to make sure you survived, more than anything else, and taking you to that convent in Nasik was the only solution we could find to save you.'

While I listen to Sakubai I think of Nirmala and I imagine her telling me that everything happened differently. I know it is impossible to get all the exact pieces of the story, but what I am finding out now seems to fit. This must have been one of the most intense episodes that Sakubai ever experienced in her life, and it is difficult to believe that she would make too many mistakes in talking about it. What reassures me most is knowing that my sister, Asha, wasn't there when they handed me over to the nuns, which is what Margaret told me in Mumbai. It was too much to bear thinking about and I put it out of my mind straight away. I am glad to hear that that scene never took place.

We don't want to say goodbye. Sakubai is like a fountain of memories and doesn't stop telling me about my mother. She has told me time and again that she was a very good woman, tolerant, affable, open – the best friend she could remember ever having had. She always wore a sari and whatever colour it was it suited her well. She didn't eat meat and the only religious practise Sakubai could remember her maintaining was that of the *ekadashi*: a Hindu ritual of fasting on the eleventh day after the full moon and the eleventh day after the new moon. A day and a half of fasting, purification before the gods with only water and tea.

Sakubai and I leave the house arm in arm. Sakubai accompanies me to the car. I walk by her side, savouring the last minutes in her company. Being with her is the closest I have ever been to my mother.

During the conversation I asked about Balu, my 'twin', and as it happens, he is the child who has turned out best in life. Sakubai and Hari had six children (four boys and two girls, the way they count). Balu was the second born. He lives in Sinnar and has a small restaurant in front of a factory where they serve food for about fifty people a day. He bought a little piece of land in front of the factory and built a house on it. He is making a good living. He works with his wife and they have no children yet. And since it is on our way, we are going to see him. Balu is a curious character in my story. He is surprised at our visit. His father, Hari, arrives with us and will spend the night there. He tells me that his documents all give the 3rd of May, 1968 as his date of birth, but that this was invented by the school administrator the first time they went to register him. In other words, we all end up the same as before, with the same collection of dates, months and years we had to begin with, which vary according to who is telling the story.

We have some tea and *pakoras* at Balu's restaurant, along with his wife. Sitting on the porch looking up at the black smoke that is coming out of the big factory chimney just across the way, I think about how I actually went a lot further than he did. But Balu is happy, and in the eyes of his family he has succeded.

7

My Sister Asha's Story

It is a splendid day in Nasik, with not a hint of rain. The convent garden in Dev-Mata is lovely. Asha and I have finally found the perfect place to spend a long time talking, explaining our lives to each other. Merlyn acts as interpreter. It is a quiet conversation between women, after all the emotion we have been through. I feel at home here and thanks to the understanding of Merlyn and the other nuns, I have invited Asha to spend a few days with me at the convent. And now here we are sitting on the stone benches in the garden, among the carefully nurtured flowers. Some of the older girls are sitting beneath the trees a little way off, revising for their exams.

'Usha!' she says to me. 'You can't imagine what it means to have you by my side. For years I had forgotten you. But since you appeared all I think about is you! I remember every minute we spent together when you came to see me the other day for the first time, after so many years of not having heard anything from you. Now we are here, in the place where you lived when you were small, where I might have lived too, and it all seems like a dream. You don't know how grateful I am that you have given me this time. I imagine that where you live now you are very busy. Just being able to spend a few days with you is fantastic, like being on holiday! It is a long time since I have slept so many hours in a row as I did last night here in the convent, in a room of my own and in a bed with a mosquito net. Ever since I was married I have only very rarely left the village, I have never gone very far from Kolpewadi. And until yesterday afternoon I had never stood on the *ghats* at the centre of Nasik! What would I do there? Who would take me? It is funny to think that you brought me there for the first time, even though I live so close by!'

When she is feeling comfortable my sister has no difficulty in talking. I have a lot of questions for her, knowing that everything she tells me could have been the story of my life. She is the other face of the moon, the other side of my story. Merlyn has quite a job translating it all because Asha talks so quickly.

'I wanted so much to see you again! I told you that I hadn't thought about you in years. With my family and the work that has to be done every day, you became very distant in my thoughts. For a time I thought you might be in Goa. You know that a lot of the nuns at the convent in Nasik are from Goa. And Goa was the furthest away I could imagine. Once, when I was grown up, I gave a photograph of myself to someone I knew who was a driver who often went to Goa in his lorry. I asked him to look out for a woman who looked like me and said that he should ask her if she was my sister, and to see if anyone might recognise me by looking at the picture. It was the only thing that I could do. The lorry driver came back with no news. This city that you say you come from, Barcelona, I have no idea where it is. You told me that it was much further away than Goa, that it takes many hours travelling in an aeroplane. But I find it difficult to imagine. Now, every time I see an aeroplane, I think of you.'

Asha looks towards the iron gate of the convent. I suppose she is imagining the same scene as I am: Sakubai and our father coming through that gate with me and little Balu in their arms.

'I was very small when our father took you to the nuns so they could take care of you. I don't remember it. It is strange to be here, in the place where they brought you! But what I do remember is the day they brought you back to the village in Shaha. I was seven years old then. I was in the field cutting grass with Baba Radhu, our father. I called him Baba or Baba Radhu. Someone came running up shouting that you had come back again. You must have been about three then. I don't know how many years there are between us. Two? Three? Four? I don't know how old I am. I don't have any paper on which it is written. At first you cried and shouted, 'sister, sister', because you wanted to go back with the nuns. Later on you calmed down. All the family came to see you. Baba Radhu cried as well. I didn't really understand what was going on. Now I know that that day was arranged so that we could say goodbye. A few days later they would take you to Mumbai. We went to the place where they burned our mother and we all prayed. Then we sat down under a tree and you sang a song. Someone took some photographs, perhaps one of the nuns: Baba Radhu and his two little girls, you and I, sitting on either side. I never saw those photographs. We were together for perhaps two or three hours. Then they took you back with them in their jeep.'

When I ask what her childhood was like, I remember clearly what mine was like in Barcelona. The weekends and all the holidays we spent in Vilanova de Prades, the village where my father comes from, where I learned how to roller skate, and the first dolls I shared with Fatima…

'I don't have any good memories of my childhood,' Asha tells me. 'Baba Radhu and I lived with Janardan's family, the only son father had left. From his first marriage he only had one son and three daughters. From the second marriage with our mother he had two sons, Dingar and Ananadar, but both of them died young, and three girls: Matura, you and me. Baba Radhu was already very old by then. He was always sad and had to work in the fields. If I didn't ask for food he wouldn't give it to me. I was a nuisance to our half-brother and his family. Janardan drank a lot, he was very violent, all of his six children were very afraid of him. But he ignored me. Baba Radhu protected me... I didn't want to do anything without him.'

'But don't you have any good memories of when you were little?' I ask her.

'One of the few good memories I have is when I played with the newly grown grass which grew after the rains, and with the mud with the other girls in the village. We would make little figures out of mud, and plates and jars, and would leave them to dry in the sun. If they didn't call us to do some kind of work or to eat, we would spend hours playing with mud. I love the warmth of the damp earth... I also remember the Diwali festivals. And also Christmas because the Jesuits and the nuns who came to the villages to bring medicine would tell us about their own festivals. I was always very impressed by those priests and nuns who used to come to our village and without knowing us at all would try to look after us and helped us so much. They had such a kind way of treating the poorest among us! No one in our village was Christian, but we thanked them for coming to see us and for helping us. I have never been baptised but ever since I was little I have felt an urge to pray to the god of those good people.'

Asha continues to tell me her story, with Merlyn translating perfectly what she says, from Marathi to a Spanish that she claims to hardly ever use but which she speaks very well, and I listen and ask, and ask and listen without stopping.

'Sometimes Baba Radhu would take me to the house of our big sister, Matura. But she had a lot of work to do, carrying firewood and fetching water. I was very young when she got married and went to live a long way away, close to Mumbai. She was never really a big sister or a mother. We spent very little time together. She gave me these holes in my ears and nose, to wear rings in, just before she left. She died far away, many many years ago now. Other times I spent some days at the house of my uncles, our mother's brothers. Pandit and Murlinder Sansare. It was nice in their house and their wives loved me very much. Our half-sister, Sakubai, and her husband, Hari, also loved me a lot and I lived at their house for many months, during some harvests. As a girl I remember moving about from one place to another, not knowing where I would end up sleeping, how many days I would stay in one house or another.'

'And school? Did you go?' I ask, knowing what kind of answer to expect.

'I never went. We were poor and in those days you had to pay to go to school. If I didn't help out with the work that had to be done I wouldn't eat. I only know how to write my name in Marathi because my daughter, Savita, showed me. Bikhaji, my husband, also learned how to write his name, the boys showed him, but he doesn't know any more than that either. My uncles wanted to send me to school, but I recall that I didn't want to go, because it would mean leaving the village, going to live with them and leaving my father. He was the only one I really felt belonged to me.'

'Baba Radhu had around two hectares of land which he had inherited from his family. We depended on the land to give us what we needed to eat. He had a horse for travelling from one village to another and three cows. The land needed a lot of work and constant attention. I helped as much as I could, because Janardan drank so much he didn't do enough work and Baba Radhu couldn't manage all by himself. This was a time of droughts, and Janardan began selling off pieces of the land, little by little, until there was nothing left of it for us. Baba Radhu was a gentle man. He never ever lost his temper with me.

He took good care of me, almost as much as a mother would. He is the only man I have ever seen take care of a girl. Here, that is quite unusual. The men don't know how to take care of children but our father did. You take after him a lot, you have the same colour skin and the same eyes. I can see that you are his daughter. My son Rahul also looks a lot like his grandfather and you in the same way. I don't remember anything about our mother. Only what people have told me.

'Baba Radhu started to have problems with his feet and legs, which grew inflamed to the point where he could no longer walk. I went with him to the doctor. They didn't know how to cure him. One day he died and I was left alone. Very, very alone. You have seen what Shaha is like. Baba Radhu was cremated in the middle of a field, in the same place where we had cremated our mother. The ashes of the two are spread on the same ground.'

I was very curious to know how she had met her husband and how they lived in the first years of their marriage. I asked questions and she began to laugh in between phrases translated by Merlyn, who was also enjoying our conversation. Asha was embarrassed to talk about certain subjects, but little by little she told me everything I wanted to know.

'I was still a little girl when my uncles, Pandit and Murlinder, started to look for a husband for me and to consider the proposals that came to them. Because I was very poor they didn't have anything to offer as a dowry. The man they found was called Bikhaji Meherkhamb, he was from Kolpewadi, a big village which I didn't know but which I knew was not very far away and was also very poor. He didn't know how to read or write either, neither of us had ever been to school. As a couple, we were perfectly balanced and everyone thought this was for the best. We met for the first time a day before our wedding. The presentation was done in Shaha, at Janardan's house. I remember perfectly well the look of surprise on Bikhaji's face when he saw me. I looked so small next to him! I was still a little girl and he couldn't hide his disappointment! He was eight or nine or ten years older than me. Neither he nor I knew exactly when we were born. We have no official document. I suppose we must figure in some register somewhere, but I don't know where. In those days the difference in years between Bikhaji and me was very obvious, he seemed much older than me! I got married in a pink sari which cost a hundred rupees. In those days that was a lot of money! My uncles arranged for my dress and my bride's necklace, which wasn't even gold. A few years later I was able to change it for a real one. The ceremony was like all the Hindu ceremonies, with lots of flowers, rice, food and music. We went to live in his village, in Kolpewadi, at his mother's house. My mother-in-law was the worst thing about my marriage. She was very mean to me and used to hit me if I did something wrong, for the slightest reason. I suffered a lot. Bikhaji was always very good to me, he always treated me with a lot of respect, like a sister. He was helpless when his mother maltreated me, because she was in charge and it was her house! Now my mother-in-law is old and everything that happened is a long way in the past.'

❦

Then all of a sudden Asha became serious. She went on with her story, after telling us that no one had ever asked her so many questions as me. It was strange for her to talk about herself.

'It was impossible for me to get pregnant, because I hadn't even started menstruating!' she tells me, looking into my eyes and half smiling. 'But even so, my mother-in-law threatened me, telling me that I would never have children, as if she wanted to put a curse on me. Three and a half years after we were married I became pregnant. You can work out how old I must have been, I always get mixed up about ages! Bikhaji and I were very happy. We all hoped it would be a boy, nobody wants to have girls. When a woman gives birth for the first time it is her own family that has to take care of everything, she has to go to her family's house. Which is why they took me to my uncle Murlinder's house in Balhegaon-Nagda, the village of the Sansare, of our mother. Murlinder's wife and Pandit's wife prepared a makeshift bed out of blankets on the floor, inside the house. I had not been seen by any doctor. I've only been to the doctor a few times. I don't like them. But the midwife did not forsee any problems.

'I gave birth for the first time just like almost all the women in our family: on the floor surrounded by other women. Without any form of anaesthesia and without being sewn up as I hear they do in the hospital. Bikhaji didn't attend, not for the first nor for the next three. How shameful it would be for him to see me like that! Sheetal was born. We were happy, even though it was a girl. But my mother-in-law was not at all pleased! I became pregnant again almost immediately. The second birth was also at the house of my uncle Murlinder and that is where Savita was born. That time neither my mother-in-law nor Bikhaji were at all happy! Several years went by before I became pregnant for the third time. Finally we had a boy! Bausaheb was born on the floor in our house in Kolpewadi, the house that you know. Yes, the whole village heard it. We are all accustomed to hearing the cries of a woman giving birth. There is no glass in the windows and we all share in each other's lives. It is difficult to do anything without the others hearing. Rahul was born two years later, also on the floor of the house. I didn't want to go to some doctor's house. Having two girls and two boys makes me feel very happy, I managed to make everyone happy.'

'Bikhaji works in the sugar cane factory in Kolpewadi, moving sacks from one place to another. Before that he worked in the fields. Now he earns more. Two thousand five hundred rupees a month. We live a very normal life, but we are not poor. I will always be grateful to my uncles, Pandit and Murlinder, for marrying me to him. He is the best husband I could ever have found. We were married very young, we knew nothing about each other, but now we love each other very much and couldn't live without one another.'

⁂

Bikhaji now seems to me to be the best husband for my sister. I find him amiable and I will always be grateful to him for allowing me to spend all these hours together with Asha. I know that if he had been against the idea I would surely not have had the chance to get as close to my sister as I am now. Husbands rule in rural India. No matter how good the relationship is between husband and wife, it is the man who always has the last word.

'For the last five years we have had two buffalo at home. Now we also have three calves. We sell the milk that we get every day at the factory where Bikhaji works and it helps us to earn a few more rupees. Bikhaji is still very surprised about your unexpected visit. I had told him that I had a younger sister named Usha, but we never imagined that you would appear again after thirty years! All this coming and going, the last few days I have spent alone here in Nasik with you, is confusing to him. But I know that he is happy because he knows that I am happy.'

'Our daughter Sheetal only attended school in Kolpewadi for a very short time. We married her very early. We went looking for a husband for her among our relations and acquaintances. Finding a husband for a girl is a great responsibility. The husband we found was young but he had had an education. They live in the village where his parents come from, not far from Pune. Now they have two little girls, Kumali is two and a half years old and Khushya is only ten months. You have met them now, they are lovely and very healthy. Sheetal did go to the doctor when she was going to give birth, and the two girls were born by Caesarean. I don't understand why.

'Savita went to school for a little longer, until she was fifteen. Now she helps with the housework and they help me with the buffalo milk, with the clothes, with the grass that has to be cut... Now we are looking for a good husband for her. We would like to marry her as soon as possible, a few months from now. We have already met three boys who have made good offers. We have to choose one of them soon. Savita will be happy with whoever we pick, she knows that we are looking for the best husband within our own limitations. She doesn't have much of an education and she doesn't earn any money, so she doesn't really have much choice. We can't afford for her to remain single and we have to take advantage of the proposals we are receiving.'

And the boys?

'My two boys don't worry me, even though my future, and Bikhaji's too, completely depends on them. They are very lively and very keen to learn. They really like going to school and we hope that when they finish they will be able to find good jobs. These days, since you turned up, they want even more to learn about things. They say they want to be like you, they want to go and live where you live, they want to learn your language. They have found your city on a map and they have worked out the distance to get there. The four children have always treated me very well. They listen to me, they don't make me angry. They are good. We are a happy family. Our children are properly registered for the simple reason that they have been to school. I am a grandmother now to two little girls, but my daughter doesn't need my help. I like to see my grandchildren from time to time. Now you are a great-aunt as well!'

Each answer to one of my questions makes it clearer what my life would have been like up until now. It is a feeling that is difficult to describe. The sensation fills me and paralyses me on this stone bench in the convent garden.

'My days are really very similar to those of other people. We all get up between five and six in the morning and all of us do the first jobs of the day. We wash and go to fetch firewood. We have tea and chapatis for breakfast. We give the buffalo water and food. I prepare food for Bikhaji to take with him to work and for the two boys for school... Our meals normally consist of chapatis with vegetables and fruit which we buy from the village market. Dhal, rice, our cereals (bajri and jawri above all), fruit... We never eat any meat, we are vegetarians. The three of them don't come back until the afternoon. Savita and I spend a lot of hours in the fields taking care of the crops, and the grass that we sow. We eat lunch together and we don't take a nap afterwards. We have to walk to the river to wash the clothes, hang them out to dry, then go back and fetch them. Then we have to go and fetch water from the well, for ourselves and for the buffalo... We have no running water at home. Luckily, the water in the well is free and we can take as much of it as we want. Now we can have electric light as well by connecting the cable to the house of a neighbour, but we are thinking of getting our own connection soon, as well as having more than one light bulb. Some of our neighbours have a television and sometimes they invite us to go over and watch a film. I have learned a lot from the television. I have seen how people live outside this village. Now I would like to watch more and pick up more. Perhaps one day the city where you live will come on!'

❄❄

And now I cannot resist asking her what she felt when she first heard that I was still alive.

'I will never forget the day when Francis Waghmere appeared at the door of the house on his motorbike, that dark blue jacket of his that is so big, and the silver helmet. It was raining. He looked like a bad man, like some kind of thief, or someone from the police. I was afraid. Bikhaji wasn't there and I was very scared. I thought this man had come to rob us, even though he insisted that if he had wanted to steal something he would not have travelled so many kilometres in the rain on his motorbike. Francis began to tell me the story of my family in such detail, knowing all the names of the people and the villages, that I became even more confused. I made a signal to Bausaheb who went running out of the house to go and fetch my husband. It was difficult to believe what he was telling me. That my little sister Usha was in Nasik and that she wanted to come and see me and that the following day she would be coming to Kolpewadi.

'Bikhaji arrived straight away. He listened to everything that Francis explained but he thought it so strange that he didn't believe a word of it. He told me that it was impossible for that girl they had left with the nuns when she was so small to suddenly appear out of nowhere. After Francis had gone we talked for a long time. Our children listened anxiously to us. The next day Bikhaji decided to take the bus to Nasik to see if it was true or if someone was deceiving us for some reason. With his cousin and another younger man he went to the convent where you lived when you were little and where Francis said that you were staying. And yes, Bikhaji saw you and confirmed that it was all true. When he came out of the convent it was dark. Before catching the bus to come back home he called our neighbour's house from a public telephone box. I came running and when I spoke to him I couldn't believe what I was hearing. You were alive! You existed! He described you very well. You are exactly as he described you that evening on the telephone!

'Bikhaji told me that we should start cleaning up the house, because the next day you and your companions would be coming to visit us. He said that I should buy biscuits and tea and that we shouldn't be short of anything and if I didn't have money I should go and ask those people who owed us money for the milk. And that is what I did, and when I had collected all the money, I went to buy some pakoras, and the ingredients I needed to make fritters, biscuits and tea.'

My life will never be the same now that I have got to know Asha. Before Merlyn can finish translating what I would like to say to her, Asha takes my hand once more and, looking at me, carries on speaking in a language which at times I pretend to understand by nodding my head.

'I have never had any great dreams or hopes, I don't expect great things, but suddenly all of that has changed. Having found you again has changed everything. I have always had a kind of anonymous life in the village and now everyone is talking about me, about my good fortune. They want to know everything about you even though I tell them I don't know all that much about you myself. Some parents with young sons want me to give them your address and telephone number so they can write and call to ask you to help them obtain a visa and work in Spain. I imagine that you can't help everyone, but I don't know what to say to them!

'The only thing I wish for now is not to lose you. And that you learn Marathi so that we can understand one another better! I don't want you to live in India, I am sure you are fine where you are, much better than you would be here. Our life is very hard, very simple. Stay where you are. I only ask one thing of you: that from time to time you call the house of my brother-in-law, Bikhaji's brother who lives a few houses further down. They will call me straight away. You speak your language and even though I won't understand, the sound of your voice would be enough to feel you near!'

8

Leaving the Land Behind

The five of us make the journey back from Nasik to
Mumbai in the white Toyota driven by Akaram.
There is an impressive monsoon downpour and
a grey light which inspires calm. We are all tired. The high
emotions of the last few days have left us all exhausted.
We hardly talk. The road passes through a green landscape
filled with cultivated terraces. From time to time a train
overloaded with people passes by, so many people that it
seems as though some of them must fall from the windows
and doors, all of which are open. How many people there
are in India! So many children everywhere!

I am getting further away from the land where I was born, from Asha, from Sakubai, from my nephews, from all the relatives who were so excited knowing that I had come back, that they had found me. The rain drums on the roof of the car. Akaram knows all the tricks to overtake the lorries, evade the bicycles, rickshaws, motorbikes, dogs, goats, and the people who walk along the side of the road under umbrellas.

Finding your biological family is not like going on an ordinary trip; it is a journey into yourself, an experience that takes time to digest. I know that things will never be the same again, not after having walked hand in hand with my sister through the fields to the place where my parents rest, or discovering that the woman who I had always thought was my mother in fact wasn't. Nothing will be the same again after learning that my father didn't abandon me a few days after I was born, but handed me over to the people he thought would ensure that I had a better life than he thought he could give me. It was the only solution once Sakubai's father-in-law refused to allow her to breast-feed me any longer. Nothing will be the same after having consoled Sakubai over the death of my mother, her friend.

Of all the things I discovered in the last few days, learning that Sitabai, my mother, did not appear in any register, any document, that she lives on only in the memory of the few people alive who knew her, has had a big impact on me. It was wonderful being able to speak to them, to hear them talk about my mother.

To tell the truth, I hadn't prepared myself to confront the experience of finding a biological sister, even less to find the woman who helped me survive by giving me her milk after my mother died. I hadn't read any books on the subject. I hadn't spoken to anyone else who had had a similar experience. I had to believe that it would work out. Now, however, I think that it wouldn't have been bad to prepare myself a little, because the flurry of ideas and sensations, contradictions and emotions that I am now returning home with is quite daunting.

❧❦

When I came back home after my first trip to India I realised suddenly that there was a whole world of mothers and fathers in the middle of the adoption process, and that perhaps they might find it useful to hear my story in order to imagine what their children would experience, and so I felt obliged to write it down. Now I am returning home thinking above all about adopted people like myself, all those people who were born in some far off corner of the world and were educated in a different culture, a different environment. I am thinking of all those people who at some point in their lives ask themselves where they come from and what happened for them to end up living with their new parents, far away from where they were born. It is those people whom I now feel I want to talk to, it is for them that I would like to tell this story of my return to the Godavari, to inspire them to look for the pieces of their puzzle much earlier than I did, and be much better prepared than I was.

If it takes too long to unravel the background trail of an adoption, it is quite possible that none of the people involved are still around. It may be that the stories you hear from different people are too far apart, or that there is simply nothing left to find, no means of information, that all the tracks have disappeared.

Many people think that it is not worth the effort, that they will not find the information they are looking for. But I would urge all those who were adopted when they were very young and might have thought of making the journey one day, maybe when they are a little older, to put aside the notion that it is not worth the effort and to take the chance of returning to their country of origin. It is worth it to find the street where you had always been told you were discovered in a cardboard box, or basket. To go to the door of the post office, or a pharmacy, or to sit on the steps of that hospital where you have been told you were left in plain sight so that you would be found right away. Once there, pause to look around you, listen to the sounds which might possibly be the ones you heard when you were very small. Look at the light in that place at different times of the day and try to imagine a father or mother who loves you but cannot take care of you for whatever reason, which unfortunately often turns out to be the case, and left you there thinking that someone would find you and give you a better life. Quite probably they were not mistaken and it has been so.

It is worth going to the gate of the orphanage where you spent the first months or years of your life and trying to get in to speak to those who work there. Try to find out if any of the people who were there at the time are still there and might remember you, or at least remember what things were like when you lived there.

The rain continues to fall as we pass through the outer quarters of Mumbai, which I recognise immediately. And without looking away from the window I think that now I feel more Indian than ever before, although curiously enough, more Catalan too. It is difficult to explain and it is not easy to find the words. I suppose that it is a feeling that I can share only with others who have been adopted, who have made a similar journey to mine, who have found important members of their natural family, who have managed to see close up, if only for a few moments, what their lives would have been like if they had not been adopted. They should remain proud and happy with the lives that they have lived with their adoptive parents, just as I am, and return home with this dual sense of belonging.

As evening falls, the bay road leading to the district of Colaba skirting the sea is jammed with cars, motorbikes and taxis sounding their horns. The vendors selling freshly cut garlands of jasmine wander between the stopped vehicles, holding their merchandise in their hands. A lot of drivers buy them to improve the air inside their cars or else to take home with them.

It has not taken another twenty years for me to come back to India, as I thought it might at the end of my first book, and now I know that it will not be as many more before I see myself reflected in the waters of the Godavari, as sacred as those of the Ganges.

Mumbai–Nasik–Barcelona, June–October 2003

Notes

End note addressed to the people in this story

Any inaccuracy in this account is due to the passage of time, which has erased some tracks that proved difficult to find. I have tried to reconstruct it from everything that was told to me, at times lending more weight to some sources than to others, but always with the best intentions.

Glossary of Indian Words

(The majority in Marathi)

Baba: Form of addressing a father or an old man to show respect and affection.

Chapati: A kind if Indian bread made of flour and water and baked on the fire, eaten with every meal.

Dhal: Typical dish in Indian cuisine that is eaten all over the country and is made of lentils with spices. It is like soup. Families with limited resources live on dhal and chapatis.

Diwali: One of the most important festivals in India, it is celebrated for five days between October and November, during which, among other things, a lot of lanterns are lit in the streets, the temples and outside the houses.

Ghandi topi: White beret that is worn by men in India, especially in the rural areas. Originally a symbol of being a follower of Ghandi and, above all, opposed to British colonisation. It continues to be a nationalist symbol but its frequent use is due to the fact that it is much more practical and comfortable than the *pheta* (turban).

Ganesh: Hindu god in the form of an elephant. It is the god most dear to the Hindus, the god of daily life.

Ghat: Stone steps that descend to the sacred rivers of India for people to do their ablutions, to say the relevant prayers, and to wash their clothes.

Pakoras: Indian snacks, which can be fritters, *samosas* (small fried pastries), meatballs, or made with vegetables and rice and other foods that are easy to make and quick to eat.

Pheta: Small turban made with a long strip of cloth, traditionally worn by all men working in the fields. Usually white in colour, but also seen in red and green.

Puja: Prayers, Hindu ritual which takes place several times a day.

Rickshaw: Taxi that can carry two or three people, consisting of a motorbike with a small cabin. In some cities the rickshaws are also bicycles that pull a small cart big enough for two people (though at times whole families can be seen being pulled by a poor driver cycling furiously).

Rupee: Indian currency. In 2003, one Euro was worth 50 Rupees; a thousand rupees is the equivalent of twenty Euros.

Saddhu: Hindu religious man dedicated to contemplation. The majority are characterised by the fact that they walk around practically naked, with long white beards and necklaces. They live on alms.

Sai Baba: Indian saint, considered a divinity by the poorest people of India. Pictures of him, an old man with a white beard, are to be found everywhere: in cars, houses, offices and so on.

Salwar kameez: Typical clothing of the countries of the Indian subcontinent (India, Pakistan, Bangladesh) which consists of trousers and a long shirt that reaches down to the feet. The men tend to wear light coloured plain cotton ones; women usually wear printed cloth and more sophisticated material.

Sari: Typical clothing of the Indian subcontinent consisting of six to nine metres of cloth (depending on the style of the sari) which is wrapped around the body above a skirt and a short blouse. They are a variety of colours and patterns, and are worn differently in each area.

Sikh: Indian religion. Sikh men are characterised by the big turbans they wear, which hide the long hair that they are not allowed to cut.

Shiwar: A term describing the outlying districts of a town, somewhere between a suburb and an area or neighbourhood.

Taluka: A collective name for a dozen or so villages in a district in one of the various states in India. Each district comprises around fifteen *talukas*.

Vasti: Small house in the rural areas built for people who work the fields or for factory hands. Normally they are owned and constructed by the same family with the help of the neighbours.

Acknowledgements

The first part of this book would not exist without the indispensible help of Gemma Sardà. She had the patience to spend hours listening to my story and helping me to structure it and give it form, to decipher the notes in my diary and rewrite those in my mother's, so that we could publish them. Thank you, Gemma, for all your dedication.

Thanks to my mother, for having started a diary for me in a notebook with red covers, when I was still in India, and later, over the years, consistently writing from day to day, to make it easier for me to understand my new life, the way it was. Thank you also for allowing me to insert a few fragments from that very personal diary into the pages of this book.

Thanks to my father for his unconditional love, with whom I feel a profound, unlimited bond. Although he does not appear too often in the pages of this book, his presence and his support have been constant since the first day.

Thanks to Fatima, my sister, for allowing me to tell her story as well, which is very closely bound to mine.

I am grateful to Anna Soler-Pont, my friend, literary agent and soul sister, for accompanying me on the second return journey to the Godavari and for being at my side at all times. Without her I don't know if I would have managed to discover all the details of my origins. Her perseverance knows no limits! I thank her also for helping me to write this book.

I am grateful to Carme Jané and Arturo San Agustin for having given me the necessary motivation to dare talk about myself.

I am grateful to Paco Escribano for having persuaded me to write, and having introduced me to Anik Lapointe, my editor, who has always had confidence in this project.

Thank you to Vicenç Altaió, friend and brother, for his sympathy and support.

I will always lack the words to fully thank Francis Waghmere. The image of him travelling around the villages surrounding Nasik on his Vespa in the monsoon rains looking for my biological family, for sentimental reasons alone, will stay with me forever.

Thank you to Jordi Llompart, Mikele Lopez and Grau Serra for being there too at my side and recording and living the most important moments of that magical voyage (with a good supply of Kleenex!). Thank you to Mikele and Grau for letting me use some of their photographs to illustrate these pages, and for their infinite support.

Thank you to Nirmala Dias, Merlyn Villoz and Margaret Fernandes for their help and all the love they gave me. Also to the sisters at the Dev-Mata convent in Nasik: Josefa, Zoe, Meena, Elsy, Stella and Kanta.

Acknowledgements

I would like to thank all of my biological family in the villages of Shaha, Kolpewadi and Ujani for receiving me with so much warmth after so many years.

Thank you to Frederic Sopeña for his hospitality in Mumbai and for his advice.

Thank you to all the people who have endured my worries and anxieties both before and after this journey. In particular I am grateful for the patience of Fatima, Ricard, Marina and Bernat.

Thank you to all the adopted people who have approached me to tell me their stories and for helping me to understand the details of my own. Also to the mothers and fathers, grandfathers and grandmothers, and all the families and friends who have experienced an adoption personally, for their support.

Asha Miró works in television and was nominated Catalan Personality of the Year in 2004 for her work on multicultural integration and international adoption. A number one bestseller in Spain, her book has sold over 150,000 copies and captivated audiences across Europe.

Also Available

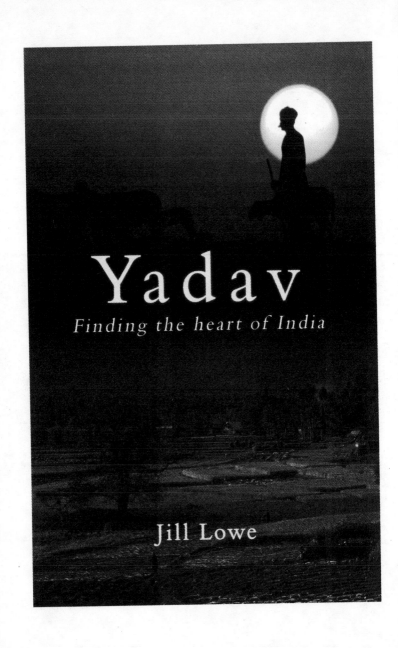

Yadav

Finding the heart of India

Jill Lowe

Yadav

Finding the heart of India

Jill Lowe

184024 056 3

'An extraordinary tale of a difficult but ultimately happy collision between two very different worlds... Remarkable, honest, funny and frequently very moving'

William Dalrymple

'This tale of life in rural India is both stark and intensely moving... This book does not give an over-romantic or sentimental view of India... this tale becomes much more than a travelogue; just as Lowe is fully immersed in Indian culture, so are we'

Wanderlust

'Ultimately, the book is about the man for whom it is named: Yadav. While the rest of the world around him – his own fellow Indians – dismiss him as a 'mere taxi driver', as if that were a caste of people whose function is to be invisible, Jill, the foreigner, the outsider, looks at him and sees a warm, loving, and lovable man. Like the best kind of documentary film, it opens doors inside the walls of our own minds and hearts, showing us what we could all find if only we bothered to look'

The Pioneer, **India**

Leaves from the Fig Tree

DIANA DUFF

Leaves from the Fig Tree

Diana Duff

184024 363 5

Raised by her eccentric grandparents at Annes Grove in County Cork, an Irish stately home famed for its beautiful gardens, Diana Duff grew up in an enchanted world of family ghosts, buried treasure and banshees. At the age of eighteen, she left in search of the excitement and freedom of fifties' Kenya.

'She writes of her years there with the candour of an honest diary and the verve of letters to an intimate friend. Her account of pioneer years teems with picturesque incidents and good humour'

The Spectator

'A most impressive first book... an extraordinary tale of extremes – from the eccentric traditions of rural Ireland to the savage beauty and desperate poverty of life in Africa. It is a beautiful tale of a life far away in time and place'

City to Cities Magazine

'a terrific read'

Sunday Times.co.za

LAURIE GOUGH

'Inspiring, funny and touching'
Isabel Losada

KISS THE
SUNSET PIG

*An American Road Trip
with Exotic Detours*

Kiss The Sunset Pig

An American Road Trip with Exotic Detours

Laurie Gough

184024 488 7

Laurie Gough drives west across the USA in a beaten-up old car named Marcia. Back in her early twenties, she discovered a secluded cave on a California beach and wants to rekindle the *joie de vivre* she had in those uncomplicated days. She recalls the adventures she's had around the world as she closes in on the land of her dreams.

'Laurie Gough manages to be both relaxed and inspiring, funny and touching, energetic and gentle all at the same time. A reassuring commentator on our bizarre world, Laurie appreciates and enjoys humanity'

Isabel Losada

'*Kiss the Sunset Pig* is elegant, funny and poignant. I couldn't bear it to end'

Polly Evans

BUTTERTEA
AT SUNRISE

A Year in the Bhutan Himalaya

BRITTA DAS

Buttertea at Sunrise

A Year in the Bhutan Himalaya

Britta Das

184024 488 7

Often seen as a magical paradise at the end of the world, Bhutan is inaccessible to most travellers. Set against the dramatic scenery of the Himalaya, this beautiful memoir reveals hardships and happiness in a land almost untouched by the West.

When Britta, a young physiotherapist, goes to work in a remote village hospital, her good intentions are put to the test amid monsoons, fleas and shocking conditions. But as she visits homes in the mountains and learns the mysteries of tantric Buddhism, the country casts its enduring spell.

Gaining insights into the traditions of this mystical kingdom, she makes friends and falls in love. Bhutan will change her life forever.

Britta Das lives in Canada with her husband and two daughters. *Buttertea at Sunrise*, her first book, has been published in Germany and the Netherlands.

the boy in the green suit

an innocent abroad in the middle east

Robert Hillman

The Boy in the Green Suit

An Innocent Abroad in the Middle East

Robert Hillman

184024 057 1

Winner of the Australian National Biography Award, 2005

'This is no ordinary travel book and it is likely that long after you turn the last page you will be wondering what Hillman is doing now or how his life proceeded after this staggering trip... It is innocence, which shines through every page of this wonderful memoir, that makes this book so rewarding and moving. This is, quite simply, a wonderful book and one to be enjoyed time and time again'

BootsnAll Travel

'The book becomes the story of physical and psychic survival, with a sub-plot around the story of Hillman's father, recreated as a strong and deeply troubled presence'

The Australian

www.summersdale.com